Grammar Skills

FOR 3RD, 4TH, 5TH GRADES

Frank B. Kamara

authorHOUSE®

AuthorHouse™
1663 Liberty Drive
Bloomington, IN 47403
www.authorhouse.com
Phone: 1-800-839-8640

First published by AuthorHouse 10/04/2011

ISBN: 978-1-4634-0723-0 (sc)
ISBN: 978-1-4634-0724-7 (ebk)

Library of Congress Control Number: 2011910018

Printed in the United States of America

Any people depicted in stock imagery provided by Thinkstock are models,
and such images are being used for illustrative purposes only.
Certain stock imagery © Thinkstock.

This book is printed on acid-free paper.

Frank Kamara, born and raised in Sierra Leone, immigrated to America to attend college to become a teacher. He received his undergraduate and graduate degrees from Indiana Central University in Indianapolis and taught elementary school in the Indianapolis Public Schools for three years and in the Metropolitan School District of Perry Township for 30 years. He has taught various grade levels but his final 28 years were taught in the 4th grade. He was coordinator of the program for gifted students for ten years. In 1995-96 Frank was named Southport Elementary and Perry Township Teacher of the Year. He received the Human Achievement Award in 2002 from the Indiana Center for Leadership Development. In 2009 he received the Perry Township Award of Merit and the Martin Luthor King, Jr. 'Focusing on the Big Picture Award'. Frank lives in Greenwood, Indiana. He has recemtly retired from teaching and he is presently writing his memoirs. He dedicates this book to his family, and all the educators in Perry Township Schools in Indiana, and especially his fellow teachers at Southport Elementary School in Perry Township.

Thank you to Mary C. Cantwell for her editorial and clerical assistance during the preparation of this book.

Contents

Sentences

A **sentence** is a group of words, arranged orderly, that makes sense, usually with a subject and a predicate. It begins with a capital letter and ends with a special punctuation mark.

There are four types of sentences:

A **declarative sentence** makes a statement and ends with a period.
> Example: Saturday is my favorite day of the week.

An **interrogative sentence** asks questions and ends with a question mark.
> Example: Where were you when I called?

An **imperative sentence** gives a command or makes a request, ends with a period, and sometimes with an exclamation mark.
> Example: Close the door as you leave.

An **exclamatory sentence** expresses strong feelings or excitement and ends with an exclamation mark.
> Example: Don't cross the street! Watch the car!

Exercise: Read the sentences below. On each line, add the punctuation mark and write the kind of sentence:

> *declarative*   *interrogative*   *imperative*   *exclamatory*

1. The baby is warm under the fuzzy blanket _____   _____

2. Please don't talk in the classroom during learning _____   _____

3. Have you ever met my sister, Britany _____   _____

4. Whoo _____ I just won the spelling bee _____   _____

5. Chan, close the door immediately _____   _____

6. George Washington was our first president _____   _____

7. Where is my orange umbrella _____   _____

8. Some restaurants serve fried worms for lunch _____   _____

9. You should clean your dirty room right away _____   _____

10. How did the poem end _____   _____

11. My mother said, "The apples are very delicious _____"   _____

12. My pet dinosaur is a big-headed monster _____   _____

13. Hurry _____ Call the fire department now _____   _____

14. Did you know that fungi and algae are plants _____   _____

15. Give me the map please, Melissa _____   _____

16. My sister eats like an elephant _____   _____

17. Walk quickly towards me, then stand still _____ _____

18. Some maple trees produce sweet syrup _____ _____

19. What a gorgeous, wonderful day _____ _____

20. These are mountains on the globe _____ _____

21. Frank thinks my little sister is prettier than me _____ _____

22. Go to bed now, Gabrielle _____ _____

23. We can hardly wait for summer to arrive _____ _____

24. What were you reading about in your novel _____ _____

25. Are you short or tall _____ _____

26. I can sing well because I have a beautiful voice _____ _____

27. My friend, Alicia, is a very nice person _____ _____

28. Did you see my uncle's brightly colored truck _____ _____

29. Sometimes we order pizza for lunch _____ _____

30. Sit down and have your dinner now _____ _____

31. Do some people *not* believe the Earth is warming _____ _____

32. Algebra is my favorite subject in fourth grade _____ _____

33. Hurray _____ My team is winning _____ _____

34. Is mother getting ready to fix our dinner _____ _____

35. Pass me the pepper, please _____ _____

36. Stop _____ You are about to step on a snake _____ _____

37. I love to visit the zoo and see my favorite animals _____ _____

38. The solar eclipse will take place tomorrow _____ _____

39. What is the name of our current President _____ _____

40. Do not take a test until you study for it _____ _____

41. Julie eats snacks after school every day _____ _____

42. The contest is over and I scored the most points _____ _____

43. Africa is a continent made up of many states _____ _____

44. Will someone listen to me when I speak _____ _____

45. The thing I fear most is flying in an airplane _____ _____

46. Did you sign your name on the dotted line _____ _____

47. My patience is running out _____ Hold your horses _____ _____

48. Earth is the third planet in the solar system _____ _____

49. Was Columbus an explorer or a historian _____ _____

50. Don't lie _____ Tell the truth _____ _____

Subject and Predicate

The **subject** in a sentence is the noun or pronoun that answers the questions: Who or what did something? The **predicate** in a sentence is the verb that answers the question: What did the subject do?

Example: The <u>teacher</u> <u>is teaching</u>.

'teacher' is the subject; 'is teaching' is the predicate

A **simple subject** is **just the noun or pronoun,** and a **simple predicate** is **just the main verb.**

Example: The <u>teacher</u> <u>is teaching</u>.

'teacher' is the simple subject;

'is teaching' is the simple predicate

A **complete subject** is **the noun or pronoun and all the words that go with the simple subject,** and a **complete predicate** is **the verb, or simple predicate and all the words that go with it to give details.**

Example: <u>The intelligent teacher with the mustache</u> <u>is teaching all the children in his class</u>.

The complete subject is 'The intelligent teacher with the mustache' which is underlined once, and the complete predicate is 'is teaching all the children in his class' which is underlined twice.

Exercise:

1. Read each sentence, draw a slash mark (/) to separate the simple subject from the simple predicate, or the complete subject from the complete predicate.

2. Write simple subject and simple predicate, or complete subject and complete predicate above the words and indicate them as such with brackets [ ].

3. Circle the (main noun) in the subject, and underline the main verb in the predicate.

      complete subject   complete predicate

1. [My brother] / [creates fantastic creatures on computers].

2. John's pet bit his nose.

3. Several boys and girls in my classroom passed the test.

4. My best friend was a famous class clown.

5. The meteorologist accurately predicted the weather.

6. Tom, Jane, and Ansu explored the tall mountain.

7. The United States of America has a powerful military.

8. My fingers and toes usually ache after gymnastics.

9. His aunt plays piano to entertain her family.

10. All people can appreciate all kinds of music if they want to.

11. Most students watch television several hours a night.

12. Early Colonists celebrated Thanksgiving with the Indians.

13. I always try to work hard in class.

14. My family takes vacations usually in the summer time.

15. Hard work and perseverance usually lead to success.

16. The teachers received instructions from their principal.

17. Our team members agreed to work together.

18. The custodians cleaned the hallway to perfection.

19. The whole group was late when the movie started.

20. The United States won more Olympic medals than any country in the world in the 2005 Olympics.

21. The fourth graders were very amused by the exhibit.

22. The humongous asteroid fell over Russia.

23. Most of my friends missed school because of the snow.

24. Several students missed the bus.

25. The small colorful bird attracts many bird watchers.

26. Tom, Mary, and Fred are expert mountain climbers.

27. We may reach the top of Mt. Everest sooner than we think.

28. My parents always paid their bills on time.

29. Thermometers measure temperatures.

30. The huge dog in the cage barks loudly all night.

31. Mary and her class mates play outside for hours on Saturdays.

32. The car race ended with no clear winner.

33. Our teacher hates lazy people.

34. The river monster catfish has attacked many humans before.

35. Both boys and girls signed up for the cheerleading team.

36. Tim and his father washed and waxed the new car.

37. The big brown bear killed a deer.

38. Bill celebrated his eleventh birthday last week.

39. Geese usually fly south in the winter.

40. Some people keep snakes as pets.

Punctuation

Punctuation is the use of certain marks to clarify meaning of written material by grouping words grammatically into sentences, clauses, and phrases; or by indicating separation of words into sentences and clauses and phrases.

Examples: period (.), comma (,), apostrophe ('), question mark (?), exclamation mark (!), quotation marks ("___") , colon (:), and semicolon (;).

A **period** is a punctuation mark (.) placed at the end of a declarative sentence to indicate a full stop at the end of a sentence or after an abbreviation.

Examples:

1. I like to watch movies.
2. Mrs. Jones visited Capt. Smith in the hospital.

A **comma** is a punctuation mark (,) that has different functions within the grammatical structure of a sentence. (Refer to page 17 for more examples.)

Example: Frank, I have a dog, a cat, three birds, and an iguana.

An **apostrophe** is the punctuation mark (') used to indicate the omission of one or more letters or a printed word, or with nouns to show ownership or possession either singular (my teacher's desk) or plural (the boys' uniforms).

Example: Now it's time to go to Suzie's house, since you couldn't go before.

A **question mark** is a punctuation mark (?) placed at the end of a sentence to indicate the asking of a question.

Example: What time do you think we ought to leave?

Do you think that it will be too early?

An **exclamation mark** is a punctuation mark (!) used after an exclamation or an interjection.

Example: Holy cow! That ball went over the fence and out of the park!

Quotation marks are punctuation marks ("___") used to attribute the enclosed text to someone else.

Example: "Shut the door when you come in." said her mother.

A **colon** is a punctuation mark (:) used after a word introducing a series or an example or an explanation (or after the salutation of a business letter).

Example: (←)

A **semi-colon** is mark of punctuation (;) used to connect independent clauses and indicating a closer relationship between the clauses than a period does.

Example: This morning I took a shower; brushed my teeth; curled my hair; and took my vitamins before I ate my breakfast

Punctuation / Capitalization

Capitalization: We capitalize the first letter in certain words in the following ways:

> at the beginning of a sentence,
>
> proper nouns,
>
> initials,
>
> abbreviations,
>
> titles,
>
> the first letter of a word in quotations, or
>
> the pronoun 'I'.

Exercise: Rewrite each sentence and capitalize where necessary.

1. mrs. j. f. kennedy visited us today.

_____

2. thank you very much mr. williams for visiting us in december.

_____

3. the month of april is usually windy and rainy.

_____

4. i live in indiana in marion county with dr. burkman.

_____

5. since thursday was thanksgiving day, southport elementary school was closed until monday

_____

6. charles lindbergh flew from new york to paris some years ago.

_____

7. martin luther king was born in atlanta, georgia.

_____

8. june, july, and august are the hottest months of the year.

_____

9. the president lives in the white house in washington, d.c.

_____

10. john wright, my friend, who lives out on shortridge rd. has read the book, the dark street.

_____

11. the planet mars is just like the planet earth in some ways.

_____

12. mom said, "i may not be able to cook dinner tonight."

_____

13. i know that canada is on the continent of north america.

_____

14. indianapolis is the capitol of indiana, located in the united states of america.

_____

15. she murmured, "don't you think we should leave now?"

_____

16. the river nile is located in egypt which is in africa.

_____

17. my family has always visited king's island in ohio every summer.

_____

18. my name is james b. dalley. i come from springfield, illinois.

_____

19. my favorite song is "blue moon" by the drifters.

_____

20. macdonald's is my favorite restaurant.

_____

21. the pacific ocean is the largest ocean on earth.

_____

22. maybe sue and her sister, jane can celebrate christmas with us?

_____

23. "yes!" she exclaimed with great excitement. "i finally made the team!"

_____

24. on tuesday we'll sail out on lake michigan for my birthday.

_____

25. scientists are observing haley's comet as it approaches planet earth.

_____

26. capt. jones is our neighbor down on melrose street.

_____

27. "mt. everest is considered by most people as the tallest mountain on earth." said frank to his students.

_____

28. john said, "this game won't be won tonight by the eagles."

_____

29. she'll leave on friday, january eighth for london, england.

_____

30. "my teacher read the book, black diamond to us," said mary.

_____

31. "what's your favorite food, james?"

_____

Combining Sentences

Two single sentences can be **combined** by using **conjunctions** and other words like: **and, but, so, because, however, nevertheless, or, etc.**

Exercise: Combine the sentences below by using the words above, and use a comma whenever it's necessary.

1. My brother likes the outdoors. I prefer to read books indoors.

_____

2. The weather is awful today. I'll try not to go outside.

_____

3. Anacondas do not chew their prey. They swallow them.

_____

4. I cannot go to the movies tonight. The show is tomorrow.

_____

5. It's raining dogs and cats. I'll take my umbrella with me.

_____

6. I failed the history test. I didn't study for it.

_____

7. Patty doesn't like to stay inside during recess. She stayed in class today to complete her homework.

_____

8. There is lot of snow on the ground. I'll go out and play in it.

_____

9. You'll either do your homework. You'll get grounded.

_____

10. John and his friend played a game of football. They were very sweaty.

_____

11. I have two favorite dolls. They are Bobby and Mandy.

_____

12. I love Hip-Hop music. My friends listen to country music all the time.

_____

13. Most people in Sub-Sahara Africa live on fish, rice, and meat. People in the North live on meat and vegetable.

_____

Punctuation: Commas

The comma is used to separate words in your writing in the following ways:

1. when making a list;

Example: I am buying hot dogs, buns, ketchup, and mustard.

2. between a city and state;

Example: I live in Arlington, Massachusetts.

3. between a date and a year;

Example: Today is February 1, 2011.

4. to separate direct quotations;

Example: Mary said, "Today is my birthday."

5. to separate two related sentences before a conjunction;

Example: I want to have a party, but I want to have hot dogs.

6. after introductory words like 'yes', 'no', 'well';

Example: Yes, we will have the party on Friday.

7. separating the name of the person we're addressing from the rest of the words in a sentence.

Example: Beverly, make sure you get a list of all her friends.

Exercise: Read the sentences below and rewrite them on a piece of paper and put in the necessary commas and other punctuation marks where they are needed:

1. Mom said "We'll leave early at sunrise "

2. I replied "I don't like winter "

3. "I want my allowance for this week " Gabe demanded

4. "Read that book " the teacher demanded

5. Mrs. Pinnow asked "Who are the winners "

6. Mom went to the store and bought some milk eggs sausage and butter

7. My birthday is August 2 1998

8. I visited London England on April fourth 2008

9. The loaf of bread is big soft and appetizing

10. The Colts played in the Super Bowl in Miami Florida

11. My time is really up but I can stay a little longer

12. Yes my mother is like a gorgeous flower

13. You may go to the restroom John

14. The Hawaiian sea was calm blue and beautiful

15. My father lives in Norfolk Virginia

16. "No I have never seen his face before " said Ansu

17. My molar is loose and I need to see the dentist

18. Kayla cried "My bones are falling apart "

19. Mr. Allen sternly asked "Where is your homework "

20. "Well you cannot play today if your homework is not done "

22. Dad commanded "Sit down and eat your spinach "

23. Angela stated "I can knock you out in a minute "

24. The boys complained "Mrs. Carroll the girls are cheating "

25. My parents protested " Don't you have any respect for your elders "

26. "Mary it's time to go to bed "

27. "My ancestors came from Africa " stated my teacher

28. Heather said "Where are my freckles gone "

29. Kassandra whispered "I may not play today "

30. "Well the moon is smiling at me "

Negatives in Sentences

Negatives are words which mean **'not'**.

Some words which are classified as negatives include: **nobody, nowhere, none, never, ever, no, not, nothing, no one, etc.**

(Other words which are considered **positives** include: **anybody, somebody, anyone, someone, anything, something, anywhere, etc.**)

Contractions that use **'-n't'** are also negatives.

Example: **isn't, aren't, wasn't, hasn't, doesn't, hadn't, weren't, don't, didn't, mustn't, shouldn't, won't, can't, couldn't, and haven't.**

Using Double Negatives

When writing we **never use two negatives** in the same sentence to indicate a negative statement. If the words **'no'** or **'not'** appear in a sentence, then you would use a positive word to follow, not a negative word.

Example: I didn't see <u>no one</u> there. --- I didn't see <u>anyone</u> there.

Exercise: Underline the negative or positive words in each sentence, and rewrite the correct sentence on the line below.

1. I won't never go to scary movies again.

_____

2. She couldn't look at none of the hideous monsters.

_____

3. There wasn't nowhere else to go when the prey tried to escape.

_____

4. The actors didn't like none of the special effects.

_____

5. I can't find no good thing to say about the lazy boy.

_____

6. Nicole didn't never play with her friends during recess.

_____

7. She had never even caused no problem in school.

_____

8. He won't go nowhere without a very careful planning.

_____

9. I haven't never met no one like like him.

_____

10. My friend didn't do nothing wrong.

_____

11. I shouldn't have never started the difficult puzzle.

_____

12. It wasn't no fun to lose my favorite pet.

_____

13. Don't never give up learning new things.

_____

14. My teacher isn't no good as a soccer player.

_____

15. My grandmother never loses nothing.

_____

16. It's true that you won't learn nothing unless you try.

_____

17. My little sister doesn't listen to nobody.

_____

18. Her family don't have no idea where she has gone.

_____

19. There is a needle on the floor I can't find nowhere.

_____

20. Isn't no one going to help me with this difficult math problem?

_____

21. There weren't enough people nowhere to rescue the dog.

_____

22. I couldn't tell nobody the secret because it was too personal.

_____

23. No one heard no noises from the dark basement.

_____

24. There isn't no restaurant in my neighborhood.

_____

25. I wouldn't mind visiting nowhere during the spring break.

_____

26. Don't you know no better than argue with your teacher?

_____

27. I haven't got no money to spend for my birthday.

_____

28. I hadn't planned to go nowhere during the heavy snowstorm.

_____

29. We couldn't have ventured nowhere if we had a guide.

_____

30. It isn't polite to interrupt nobody while they're speaking.

_____

31. We ain't going nowhere fast!

_____

2 Parts of Speech

Nouns

A **noun** is the name of a person, a place, an object, an animal, or an idea. Example: Mary Jones, Indianapolis, furniture, dog, love, etc.

Kinds of Nouns

Proper nouns are the names of specific and important names of persons, places, or things. This category includes the names of people, holidays, months, days, planets, important rivers, mountains, lakes, titles, buildings, countries, continents, oceans, states, etc. **A proper noun is capitalized.**

> Example: Planet Earth, River Nile, Saturday, James, July, Christmas, White House, etc.

Common nouns are the names of ordinary persons, places, objects, animals or ideas which are not proper nouns.

> Example: planet, river, day, boy, month, holiday, house, etc.

Noun suffixes are words with suffixes that act as nouns as they are used in sentences.

> **Suffixes** are: **-or, -er, -ic, -ist, -ism, -ian, -ion, -dom, -ance, -ence, -hood, -ment, -ness, -ship**

Exercise: Put the following nouns into the columns below where they belong.

Mt. Everest	computer	creator	Thanksgiving
salt	Ohio	friendship	bravery
television	movie	carpet	pianist
confidence	creator	provider	kindness
sprinkler	Avon Street	magician	Tom Sawyer
Kroger	education	dust pan	sickness
Crayola	love	Monday	artist
Henry Morgan	mirror	basement	heroism
Africa	bench	freedom	wallpaper
allowance	Fourth of July	activism	team
desk	kingdom	adulthood	citizenship
earphones	AMC	"Titanic"	Indianapolis
operator	Jupiter	grasshopper	patience
sunlight	Mississippi River	cat	Indian Ocean
kingdom	Sgt. Smith	Lake Michigan	tunic
fireman	wolf	pianist	relationship
donation			

Common Nouns	Proper Nouns	Nouns With Suffixes

Singular and Plural Nouns

Singular nouns name one person, place, object, animal or idea. A singular noun can be common or proper.

Plural nouns name more than one person, place, object or idea. Plural nouns can be common or proper.

Rules for changing singular nouns to plural nouns.

1. Nouns to which you simply add an 's'.

    Example: book---books, fluff---fluffs, belief---beliefs

2. Nouns ending with -sh, -ch, -x, -s, and –z, you simply add 'es'.

    Example: dish---dishes, church---churches, box---boxes, dress---dresses, buzz---buzzes

3. Nouns ending with 'y'.

When the word ends with a '-y' (preceded by a consonant), you change the 'y' to 'i' and add 'es'. When the word ends in '-y' (preceded by a vowel), you simply add an 's'.

    Example: folly---follies, turkey---turkeys

4. Nouns ending with consonant-f or –fe, you change the 'f' to 'v' and add 'es'.

    Example: shelf---shelves, wife---wives

5. Nouns ending with the vowel 'o' (preceded by a consonant), simply add 'es'.

    Examples: hero---heroes,   mango---mangoes,   hello----helloes

6. Certain nouns change their structure when forming their plurals.

    Example: mouse—mice, goose---geese

7. Certain nouns do not change at all to form their plurals.

   Example: deer---deer

EXERCISE: Write the plurals for the following nouns:

1. desk _____
2. sandwich _____
3. student _____
4. leader _____
5. money _____
6. tiger _____
7. wife _____
8. circus _____
9. trouble _____
10. bus _____
11. fox _____
12. wish _____
13. child _____
14. potato _____
15. hobby _____
16. goat _____
17. man _____
18. branch _____
19. glass _____
20. deer _____
21. hero _____
22. elf _____
23. buzz _____
24. picture _____
25. dinosaur _____
26. dwarf _____
27. kiss _____
28. tooth _____
29. moose _____
30. antique _____
31. country _____
32. cousin _____
33. donkey _____
34. scarf _____
35. sheep _____
36. knife _____
37. tax _____
38. woman _____
39. chief _____
40. boss _____
41. goose _____
42. igloo _____
43. rabbit _____
44. snicker _____
45. lunch _____
46. leaf _____
47. foot _____
48. mongoose _____
49. mango _____
50. eyelash _____

Possessive Nouns

Possessive nouns are nouns that show ownership.

Rules for changing nouns to possessive nouns.

1. Add an apostrophe -'s to a singular noun to make it a possessive noun.

    Example: the dog's paws, the man's hand

2. Add an apostrophe after the - s' to a plural noun to make it a possessive noun.

    Example: many students' books, the boys' bikes

3. Add an apostrophe and an -'s to plural nouns that do not form their plurals with an 's'

    Example: men's clothes, women's makeup

EXERCISE: Write the possessive nouns for each singular or plural noun.

    Example 1. The drum belongs to the boy. <u>the boy's drum</u>
    Example 2. The secrets are my friends. <u>my friends' secrets</u>
    Example 3. Those shoes are for men. <u>men's shoes</u>

1. This dress belongs to my sister. _____

2. The hat belongs to a firefighter. _____

3. The home belongs to my parents. _____

4. Brittany owns the wig. _____

5. The books belong to the teachers. _____

6. My uncle owns the cabin. _____

7. This is a picture of a cat. _____

8. Those nests are made by birds. _____

9. The phones are for the secretaries. _____

10. This restroom is for women. _____

11. The tools belong to the dentist. _____

12. The balls belong to the players. _____

13. This area is reserved for those people. _____

14. These horns belong to the deer. _____

15. The fishing pole belongs to John. _____

16. The wagons are for the oxen. _____

17. The driver owns the racecar. _____

18. Those are the voices of girls. _____

19. This office belongs to the Principal. _____

20. The desk belongs to Ben. _____

21. The museum is for children. _____

22. The special food is for elephants. _____

23. The big shoes belong to the construction worker. _____

24. The bucket belongs to the gardener. _____

25. That food is for mice. _____

26. The jerseys belong to the teams. _____

27. The cadets own the hats. _____

28. The flight path belongs to the geese. _____

29. The dishes belong to the cooks. _____

30. The instructor owns the pencil. _____

31. The playground is for little children. _____

32. My father owns this motorcycle. _____

33. This big head belongs to Ryan. _____

34. The directions are for adults. _____

35. That cage belongs to a lion. _____

36. The chairs belong to six families. _____

37. The bandage belongs to the nurse. _____

38. The supplies belong to all the schools. _____

39. A lady owns the flowers. _____

40. Those webs belong to spiders. _____

Irregular Plural Nouns

Irregular nouns are not made plural in the same way that regular nouns are. An irregular noun will have changes in the structure of the word or it will be a new word completely.

Example: goose --- geese; mouse --- mice

Exercises:

A. After your classroom lesson about irregular nouns, write the plural nouns for the following nouns:

1. goose _____

2. mouse _____

3. tooth _____

4. child _____

5. woman _____

6. foot _____

7. ox _____

8. louse _____

9. man _____

10. sheep _____

11. deer _____

12. mongoose _____

13. moose _____

B. Write good sentences using the plural nouns above for the singular nouns below.

1. goose

_____

2. mouse

_____

3. tooth

_____

4. child

_____

5. woman

_____

6. foot

_____

7. ox

_____

8. louse

_____

9. man

_____

10. sheep

_____

11. deer

_____

12. mongoose

_____

13. moose

_____

Regular and Irregular Nouns

Exercise: Read each sentence and circle the (noun) that correctly fits in the sentence:

1. Donna has some _____ in her hair.
    a. louses   b. lices
    c. lice   d. louse

2. Most _____ wear high-heel shoes for special occasions.
    a. womans   b. women
    c. womens   d. woman

3. Several _____ on the playground are playing kickball.
    a. childs   b. childrens
    c. child   d. children

4. A _____ can be a very dangerous animal.
    a. mongoose   b. mongooses
    c. mongosse   d. mongoos

5. My father set up a trap to catch few _____ .
    a. mouse   b. mouses
    c. mice   d. mices

6. Those shoes do not fit her _____ .
    a. foots   b. foot
    c. feets   d. feet

7. _____ are animals of the horse family.
    a. oxes   b. oxs
    c. oxen   d. ox

8. Humans use their _____ to chew, tear, and crush their food.
    a. teeth   b. tooths
    c. teeths   d. tooth

9. All the workers at the construction site are _____.
    a. men   b. mans
    c. mens   d. man

10. It's not unusual to see _____ flying south during the winter.
    a. gooses   b. geese
    c. geeses   d. goose

11. The _____ roam freely in the valley below the mountains.
    a. sheep   b. sheeps
    c. shepe   d. sheepe

12. _____ are warm-blooded animals.
    a. Moongoose   b. Mongoose
    c. Mongooses   d. Moongoose

Noun Signals or Noun Determiners/Modifiers

Noun signals or **noun determiners** warn or signal that a noun may come after them when they appear in a sentence. However, they can be placed anywhere in a sentence.

They include the following words: **the, this, a, that, an, those, several, many, most, few, these, some, and any number used in a sentence**

Some of the above words should be used appropriately with singular nouns.

    Example: This game will end sooner.

Some of the above words should be used with plural nouns.

    Example: Several students passed the test.

If the noun that immediately follows a noun signal begins with a vowel, the noun signal, 'a' would be changed to 'an'.

    Example: I ate a banana. I ate an apple.

        She has a raincoat. She needs an umbrella.

Exercise: Use the noun signals/determiners given below and write a good sentence. Draw a line under the <u>noun signal/determiner</u>. Circle the (noun) they signal.

1. a _____

2. the _____

3. this _____

4. some _____

5. an _____

6. many _____

7. that _____

8. those _____

9. few _____

10. these _____

11. several _____

Pronouns

A **pronoun** is a word that is used in a place of one or more nouns. Pronouns are not nouns. They are a substitute for nouns.

There are four types of pronouns:

1. **Personal pronouns** refer directly to a person or a thing.
They include the following words:
singular pronouns: I (always capitalized), me, you, he, him, she, her, it; plural pronouns: we, us, you, they, them

2. **Possessive pronouns** show ownership by a noun.
They include the following words:
my, mine, your, yours, his, hers, its, our, ours, their, theirs

3. **Reflexive or 'self' pronouns** end with the suffix 'self'.
They include the following words:
myself, yourself, yourselves, herself, himself, itself, ourselves, themselves

4. **Indefinite pronouns** do not represent any specific noun.
They include the following words:
anyone, anybody, anything, everyone, everybody, everything, someone, somebody, something

Exercise: Use the following pronouns in good sentences. In each sentence, underline the pronoun. Above the pronoun note whether the pronoun is personal, possessive, reflexive, or indefinite.

1. herself _____

2. me _____

3. they _____

4. mine _____

5 someone _____

6. I _____

7. you _____

8. ourselves _____

9. himself _____

10. their _____

11. our _____

12. yourselves _____

13. itself _____

14. he _____

15. her _____

16. it _____

17. theirs _____

18. everybody _____

19. us _____

20. them _____

21. anyone _____

22. his _____

23. its _____

24. himself _____

25. everyone _____

26. themselves _____

27. she _____

28. something _____

29. him _____

30. my _____

31. your _____

32. anybody _____

33. her _____

34. someone _____

35. myself _____

36. yours _____

Verbs

A **verb** is an action word that shows what a person, place, or thing has done, is doing, or will do. To clarify which action is demonstrated in the sentence, verbs are classified by **tense**.

Forming Tenses

The **present tense** denotes an action that is occurring in the present.
    Example: We always <u>play</u> at recess.

Present tense can also be expressed using a helping verb in the **continuous tense**. These include **verbs 'of being': am, are, be, can, do, does, has, have, was, were, is.**
    Example: We <u>are playing</u> hide and seek.

Verbs in the **past tense** indicate that the action has already happened a time ago. Verbs in the **continuous tense** indicate that the action is happening now and not over yet. Verbs in the **future tense** indicate that the action has not happen yet, but will happen sometime later.

Rules for **changing present to past tense:**
I. To simple verbs, you simply ad 'ed' to the present tense to form the past tense.
    Example: walk --- walked

2. To verbs that end with an 'e', you drop the 'e' from the present tense, and add the 'ed' to form past tense.

    Example: dance --- danced

3. To verbs in the present tense that end with a 'consonant-y', you change the 'y' into an 'i' before adding the 'ed' to form the past tense.

    Example: hurry --- hurried

4. In most single syllable verbs, with short vowel sounds, the last consonant will be doubled before adding the 'ed'.

    Example: drop --- dropped

5. Some verbs will change as they change to past tense.

    Example: take --- took

6. Certain verbs will remain the same as they form past tense.

    Example: put --- put

If an action took place in the past, we say that the verb is **past tense**.

    Example: We <u>played</u> a game of hide and seek last week.

Certain verbs accompany past tense verbs, helping verbs, or **past participle**.
These include: **did, was, were, had, would, could, should.**

    Example: We <u>had played </u>a game of hide and seek last week.

If an action has not happened or will happen in the future, we use **future tense**. Helping verbs for future tense include: shall, will, may, might.

    Example: We <u>will play</u> hide and seek tomorrow.

Exercises:

A. <u>Underline</u> the main verb in each sentence. Circle the (helping verb.) Write on the line whether the verb is in the *present tense*, *past tense*, *continuous tense*, *future tense*, or in the *past participle*.

1. Boa constrictors squeeze their prey to kill it.

_____

2. The Sahara Desert is located in Africa.

_____

3. We visited the Pyramids on our Egyptian vacation.

_____

4. Grandmother will come to our house for Christmas.

_____

5. I am sifting through the sand to find a rare rock.

_____

6. Many guests have arrived for the wedding.

_____

7. He sat quietly while the program progresses.

_____

8. A busload of students has left for the fieldtrip.

_____

9. Many construction workers train for their career.

_____

10. We shall fly on a huge jet plane to Australia.

_____

11. She is making a raffia basket for her mother.

_____

12. Please sit down quietly.

_____

13. The heavy snow covers the ground.

_____

14. The train has crashed near the bridge.

_____

15. Jimmy and Nancy murmured in my ear.

_____

16. She viewed the eclipse for an hour.

_____

17. Training to be an astronaut is extremely difficult.

_____

18. You don't understand how to solve the problem.

_____

19. Maybe we can climb this mountain.

_____

20. I feel great today.

_____

21. We all make fun of her.

_____

22. I could throw a ball through the hoop.

_____

23. The food smells delicious.

_____

24. Tony is craving pizza.

_____

25. He escapes the mudslide .

_____

26. The asteroid had fallen on the Earth.

_____

27. Eating fruits is healthy for the body.

_____

28. Jimmy can jump the pole vault.

_____

29. We should appreciate what we have.

_____

30. Please put your seat belt on.

_____

31. The window seal is broken.

_____

32. I will be a pilot someday.

_____

33. My teacher writes children's novels.

_____

34. The Smiths may be traveling to Boston tomorrow.

_____

35. I have always taken a nap at midday.

_____

36. I will be a candidate for beauty queen next year.

_____

37. He doesn't care to brush his teeth every day.

_____

38. We always checked on our mail last year.

_____

39. My parents invited the entire team to our house.

_____

40. The rotten fruit tastes awful.

_____

41. We will enjoy the trip when we make it next week.

_____

42. The tall trees whistled as the wind blew fiercely.

_____

43. Ten years from now, I will turn twenty-one.

_____

44. The music sounds calming.

_____

45. Could you please help your mother?

_____

46. You should behave yourself during the party.

_____

B. Fill in the columns with the correct verb tenses for the regular verbs below.

PRESENT	CONTINUOUS	PAST	PAST PARTICIPLE	FUTURE
talk				
move				
jump				
fix				
organize				
cook				
mail				
miss				
visit				
whisper				
vanish				
assign				
address				
yearn				
wait				
unite				
settle				
trick				
remain				
request				
finish				

PRESENT	CONTINUOUS	PAST	PAST PARTICIPLE	FUTURE
direct				
learn				
ask				
pitch				
call				
operate				
report				
lecture				
allow				
succeed				
argue				
allow				
see				
try				
use				
fly				
hurry				
flip				
worry				
create				
bring				
grin				

PRESENT	CONTINUOUS	PAST	PAST PARTICIPLE	FUTURE
sing				
stop				
chase				
empty				
bring				
grab				
advance				
study				
shoot				
help				
go				
eat				
sit				
move				
draw				
shut				
swim				
want				
dine				

Irregular Verbs

Irregular verbs are verbs that do not follow the usual rules for changing tenses.

The rules for irregular verbs can be stated as:

1. Certain verbs do not add -ed to form their tenses. Their forms and spelling change as they move through the continuous, past, past-participle, and future tenses.

Example: give, am giving, gave, have given, will give

2. Certain verbs with short vowels double the last letter of the word to form their continuous or past tenses.

Example: stop, stopping, stopped

Exercise: Write the correct tenses under the columns for the following irregular verbs.

Note that the participle may use linking or helping verbs to form their tense.

Follow the rules above. Example below:

PRESENT	CONTINUOUS	PAST	PARTICIPLE	FUTURE
drive	am driving	drove	have driven	will drive
see				
drink				
slip				
begin				
speak				
become				
stop				
pin				
give				
meet				
wrap				
make				
rub				
give				
clap				
teach				
buy				
catch				
break				
tell				
sing				

PRESENT	CONTINUOUS	PAST	PARTICIPLE	FUTURE
eat				
rise				
drink				
rip				
swim				
beg				
stand				
find				
rob				
tag				
think				
hem				
fight				
grin				
cry				
grow				
dim				
take				
drive				
bring				
fly				
sell				

Helping Verbs

Linking or helping verbs are not really action words.

- They help the main verb in the predicate of the sentence so that the sentence in which they appear makes sense, and is grammatically correct.
- They are often used when changing from present to continuous, past, participle or future tense.
- They can be used to connect the subject with a noun or adjective in the predicate.

    Example: John and Jimmy <u>were trying</u> to save the injured bird.

Linking verbs are: **am, are, be, can, do, does has, have, was, were, is, did, was, were, had, would, could, should, shall, will, may, might.**

Exercise: Read each sentence. Circle the ⟨helping verb⟩ or the ⟨linking verb,⟩ and <u>underline</u> the main verb:

1. Lion puppies may learn some hunting tricks from their parents.

2. The family is planning a huge Christmas party.

3. The principal has given us permission to leave.

4. I am keeping the speed limit as I drive through the school zone.

5. Success will come to those who work hard.

6. We were packing up when the tornado hit.

7. The astronauts could fix the telescope before returning to Earth.

8. Our teacher was watching us as we took the test.

9. Shall we say goodnight to our parents before going to bed?

10. We should take our lunch with us to school.

11. Mary had just boarded the plane before they closed the door.

Continuous Tense

Forming the continuous tense: Adding the verb suffix **'-ing'** to verbs that end with the letter 'e' .

Rule: Remove the letter 'e' at the end of the word before you add the suffix "ing" to create the new word.

Example: make --- making; freeze --- freezing;

come --- coming

Exercise: Add the suffix "ing" to the following verbs and write them on the line.

1. bike _____   2. arrive _____

3. take _____   4. announce _____

5. write _____   6. hide _____

7. drive _____   8. fake _____

9. crave _____   10. terminate _____

11. move _____   12. inhale _____

13. joke _____   14. imagine _____

15. manage _____   16. frame _____

17. have _____   18. rotate _____

19. divide _____   20. challenge _____

21. meddle _____

22. please _____

23. care _____

24. glare _____

25. hike _____

26. ride _____

27. operate _____

28. poke _____

29. rate _____

30. state _____

31. wake _____

32. abbreviate _____

33. glide _____

34. formulate _____

35. date _____

36. move _____

37. create _____

38. operate _____

39. dictate _____

40. manage _____

41. rate _____

42. forgive _____

43. judge _____

44. investigate _____

45. waste _____

46. navigate _____

47. irritate _____

48. allocate _____

49. ignite _____

50. vibrate _____

51. bite _____

52. organize _____

53. name _____

54. advertise _____

Adjectives

An **adjective** is a word that describes a person, place, object, or a thing (a noun or a pronoun.) Adjectives are **describing words**. They compare nouns/pronouns in the **comparative form** and in the **superlative form**.

Rules for adjectives:

1. Adjectives can be simple descriptive words to which you add the suffixes '-er' to create the comparative form, and '-est' to make the superlative form.

    Example: high --- higher --- highest,

             smooth --- smoother --- smoothest,

             long --- longer --- longest

2. Other adjectives that end with certain suffixes are usually preceded by the words 'more' to express the comparative form, and 'most' for the superlative form.

These suffixes are: **'-able', '-ible', '-some', '-ful', '-ish', '-less', '-er', '-est', '-ive', '-ous', '-al', '-ic', or '-ary'. (There may be exceptions to this rule.)**

    Example: faithful --- more faithful --- most faithful

             desirable --- more desirable --- most desirable

3. Adjectives that end with a 'consonant-y' will change the 'y' to an 'i' before you add the '-er' and the '-est.'

    Example: pretty --- prettier --- prettiest

4. Certain adjectives with short vowels will double the final consonant before adding the '-er' and '-est' when forming their comparative and superlative forms.

    Example: big --- bigger --- biggest

5. Others go with the words 'worse' and 'worst.'

Example: I had the worst time in my life.

6. Others change completely in their comparative and superlative forms

Example: good -- better -- best

Exercise: Write the comparative and the superlative forms for the following adjectives:

ADJECTIVE	COMPARATIVE	SUPERLATIVE
tall		
frequent		
hot		
gorgeous		
hopeful		
old		
monstrous		
warm		
gifted		
horrible		
funny		
bold		
thrilled		
comfortable		
busy		

ADJECTIVE	COMPARATIVE	SUPERLATIVE
fat		
miserable		
careless		
smart		
fresh		
heavy		
hefty		
handsome		
young		
strange		
big		
robust		
good		
sad		
little		
wet		
green		
likeable		
childish		
bright		
flat		
enthusiastic		

ADJECTIVE	COMPARATIVE	SUPERLATIVE
dreary		
cute		
dull		
awesome		
active		
toxic		
merry		
well		
many		
bad		
accidental		
aggressive		
witty		

Adverbs

An **adverb** is a word that modifies, explains, or tells more about the action of a verb. It usually answers the questions:
how?, when?, or where? the action takes or took place.

Example: (how?) He drank the milk noisily.

(when?) The President's plane will land soon.

(where?) It is over there.

You can form adverbs from adjectives. Almost all 'how' adverbs end with '-ly', except the word 'often'.

Example: quick --- quickly, sweet --- sweetly

Exercise: Circle the adverbs and write on the line whether the adverb tells: how?, when?, or where?.

1. The students returned quickly to their rooms at the Principal's order.

_____

2. Soon, everyone in the building will exit because of the earthquake.

_____

3. My parents visit the old restaurant often for their anniversary.

_____

4. It took him many years to learn how to easily fly a plane.

_____

5. The rescuers in the helicopter diligently hover it over the cave.

_____

6. The car plunged fifty feet below the isolated lake.

_____

7. Few people ever attempt to explore life in the ocean's deeps.

_____

8. The party goers are leaving now.

_____

9. She hid beneath the blanket after being caught stealing cookies.

_____

10. Driving outside during a snowstorm can be very dangerous.

_____

11. She successfully extinguished the fire before calling for help.

_____

12. Grandmother often visits us because she misses us.

_____

13. The crowd cheered loudly after a very contested game.

_____

14. He slowly approached the lizard and grabbed its tail.

_____

15. We stayed inside during the heavy snow.

_____

16. We can go outside now because the tornado has passed.

_____

7. My friends will be here to celebrate my birthday.

_____

18. They will arrive at noon.

_____

19. When they get here, they'll quickly set up the stage for the music.

_____

20. The stage will be at the second level below the house.

_____

21. The party will take place right here in my home.

_____

22. Our party will start before the bad weather begins.

_____

23. Often, we think that all snakes are poisonous when they're not.

_____

24. Yesterday was my mother's birthday.

_____

25. The jet plane is flying above the clouds. This scares me.

_____

26. Kids must not automatically assume that all adults are wrong.

_____

27. "All payments must be made frequently!" demanded the owner.

_____

28. We should respond urgently to his letter.

_____

29. They can go somewhere if they don't like it here.

_____

30. Tomorrow is a special day because it's my dad's birthday.

_____

31. The great movie depicts time beyond our time.

_____

32. Why can't you stand between me and the next person in line?

_____

33. Stand there while we sing the National Anthem.

_____

Conjunctions

Conjunctions are words or group of words that join or combine words, phrases, group of words or sentences.

They include the following words: **but, because, and, or, either, however, nevertheless, for, on the other hand, though, although, for this reason.**

Exercise: Put an appropriate conjunction in the blank space in each sentence:

1. The River Nile moves north _____ the Mississippi sails south.

2. I was not invited for the party _____ I'll attend it anyway.

3. He put on his boots _____ its snowing heavily outside.

4. Jessica cannot stand on her right leg _____ it's broken.

5. Jane dyed her hair blonde _____ she could not impress her new friends.

6. The television is out _____ the electricity was disconnected.

7. It's raining _____ my mother carried an umbrella.

8. Greg's father found a new job _____ the family moved away.

9. He cut down the tree _____ he planted another one.

10. I am always having lice infestation _____ I shaved my head.

11. Saturn has many rings around it _____ Earth doesn't have any.

12. Either you choose pink as your favorite color _____ you select yellow.

13. He studied very hard for the test _____ he failed on it.

14. The fire truck roared down the street _____ put out the raging fire.

15. _____ the problem was very simple, he could not solve it.

16. I didn't obey the school rules _____ I was suspended from school.

17. Most animals are carnivores _____ others herbivores.

18. My teachers are computer literate _____ can do anything on a computer.

19. We must analyze the problem _____ solve it accordingly.

20. He was late for school this morning _____ he missed the bus.

21. Today is a holiday _____ I'll stay home.

22. _____ you apologize for your bad behavior or face the consequences.

23. Jane is a small girl _____ her brother is very tall.

24. He drove the car without brakes _____ he got into an accident.

25. No deer _____ antelopes live in this forest.

26. Some people have reached the peak of Mt. Everest _____ it's dangerous.

27. My grandfather is very old _____ he acts like a young person.

28. If you exercise every day you'll feel young _____ healthy.

Prepositions

Prepositions are words that link or connect nouns, pronouns, and other phrases to other words in sentences. Some prepositions can also be used as adverbs. Some prepositions are listed below in alphabetical order.

Example: of the boy, from my mother, at another time

A	B	D	E	F
about	before	despite	except	for
above	behind	down		from
across	below	during		
after	beneath			
against	beside			
around	between			
at	beyond			
along	but			
among				

I	L	N	O	P
in	like	near	outside	past
inside			of	
into			off	
			on	
			onto	
			out	
			over	

S	T	U	W
since	till	up	with
	through	under	within
	throughout	upon	without
	to	underneath	
	toward		

Exercise: Read each sentence, underline the <u>preposition</u>, and circle the (noun) or (pronoun) it connects.

   Example: The (child) crawled <u>beneath</u> the (couch.)

1. Jared threw the ball over to Elijah.

2. My teacher is leaning against the tall pole.

3. My little brother mourns over his cat's death.

4. Seth was unhappy after his team lost the game.

5. The vacationers climbed the tall tree without fear.

6. She decided to read the book during recess.

7. Taylor stood motionless beside the captain.

8. The poisonous spider crawled slowly under Isaac's pillow.

9. I always search my messy room for my homework.

10. There was celebration throughout the United States during the Independence Day weekend.

11. The dog is hiding under the bed to avoid his angry owner.

12. She hid behind the door after she stole the cookies.

13. Ryan placed the broken tooth on the table.

14. It's wrong to come to school without your homework.

15. Diana accidentally jumped into the river where the crocodiles were waiting to make a feast out of her.

16. Matthew showed up in the party even though he was uninvited.

17. His crooked toe got trapped under the door.

18. The swimmer surfed near some dangerous sharks.

19. Frank did all his homework except math.

20. What goes around comes around any day.

21. Frances sat on the dog's head.

22. James cannot keep his head under the water for even two minutes.

23. Water makes up about 65 percent of the human body.

24. Falling stars streaked the sky above.

25. We all gathered around the camp fire.

Prepositional Phrases

A **prepositional phrase** is a group of words or a phrase that begin with a preposition and usually ends with a noun or pronoun.

    Example: of the city; toward the river; with his mother

Exercise: Underline <u>the prepositional phrase</u> in each sentence below:

1. The weather around our state is very awful today.

2. Those pencils under the table belong to me.

3. The distance from Earth to the sun is about 93 million miles.

4. She walked along with the camels in the hot sands of Sahara Desert.

5. We will arrive at the concert on time.

6. He became sleepy during the boring movie.

7. The trained dog is loyal to its owner.

8. Some people enjoy eating popcorn at a movie.

9. At the fair, we bought some souvenirs.

10. Before the seasonal game started, the players put on their uniforms.

11. We will meet you around noon today.

12. The smoke inside the room is choking the babies.

13. The elephant rubbed his back against the huge tree.

14. She was warned to stay within the court during the game.

15. Throughout his life, James was a very kind man.

16. Living things cannot live without water.

17. He threw the ball through the small hoop.

18. You can go out for recess except those who failed on the test.

19. She has been sad since she lost her favorite dog.

20. Although he is just three years old, he sat among the adults.

21. Jonna was told by his teacher to go to the office.

22. He didn't see the snake as it crawled beneath the table.

23. My parents invited my friends to come over for dinner.

24. I was really fascinated by his charm.

25. His novel was made into a movie

26. The racecars took off as fast as they could when the signal was given.

27. Maybe we can resume the game after the rain stops.

28. The story is about how the anaconda killed its prey.

29. We will see beyond the valley.

30. The race will start within the hour.

31. Don't move towards the scared cat.

32. The prayer meeting will continue till midnight.

33. Unlike my sister, I like pizza.

Interjections

Interjections are words that express feelings.

Some interjections express strong feelings and are followed immediately by an exclamation mark and should begin with a capital letter.

The following words are examples that can be determined as interjections: **Wow! Oh! Hey! Hurray! Ah! Alas! Ouch! Ha!;** sometimes words like: **Help! Stop! Hurry! Run!;** and sometimes simple commands express strong feelings: **Go! Yap!**

Other interjections that express soft feelings are followed by a comma and an exclamation mark at the end of the sentence.

Example: Hey, don't jump in the traffic in front of those cars!

Exercises:

A) Rewrite the sentences below and put in the correct punctuations (comma, capital letters, exclamation marks, periods) after the interjections.

1. hurry our bus has just arrived

_____

2. oh I made a serious mistake

_____

3. help somebody is running away with my purse

_____

4. ouch I just hit my finger with a hammer

_____

5. hurry we are already very late

_____

6. wow my experiment actually does work

_____

7. hey why didn't you show up for the game

_____

8. stop you shouldn't cross the railroad track

_____

9. ah that doesn't make any sense

_____

10. bingo I just matched all the numbers

_____

11. sit down and be quiet

_____

12. run a lion is chasing us

_____

B) Write your own sentences using the above interjections.

1. _____

2. _____

3. _____

4. _____

5. _____

6. _____

7. _____

8. _____

 # Analogies

Analogies are a set of words which have a special relationship. The relationship between the first set of words should help you to determine the relationship between the second set of words.

Analogies can
- help you to process information,
- identify relationships between ideas and content, and
- improve your understanding of reading materials.

     Example: finger is to nail as eye is to lash.

Exercise: Write the correct word on the line from the word bank to complete the analogy below.

WORD BANK

tricycle	never	desert	joey	air pressure	boots
green	coop	sprint	humongous	octagon	yellow
scale	mane	cheese	dust cloth	wheat	continent
unattractive	2	symphony	Southern Hemisphere		3
paper	bee hive	scarf	shovel	wind	winter
screws	hexagon	ocean	boisterous	adverb	fully
author	preacher	hurricane	sweeping	Sahara	ugly
preach	temperature	vane	milk	January	crawl
composer	respiratory system				

1. Cow is to calf as kangaroo is to _____.

2. Love is to hate as always is to _____.

3. _____ is to music as artist is to painting.

4. Bicycle is to two wheels as _____ is to three wheels.

5. China is to country as _____ is to desert.

6. Silence is to quiet as noisy is to _____.

7. Person is to home as chicken is to _____.

8. Odometer is to speed as barometer is to _____.

9. Morning is to afternoon as _____ is to walk.

10. Pail is to pale as main is to _____.

11. Hands is to gloves as neck is to _____.

12. Eerie is to spooky as gigantic is to _____.

13. Tree is to _____ as wheat is to bread.

14. Wind direction is to windvane as _____ is to thermometer.

15. Narrow is to wide as gorgeous is to _____.

16. _____ is to winter as June is to summer.

17. Dust cloth is to dusting as broom is to _____.

18. Story is to _____ as poetry is to poet.

19. _____ is to bees as nest is to ants.

20. Red is to stop _____ is to go.

21. _____ is to adverb as cupboard is to noun.

22. Africa is to _____ as Pacific is to ocean.

23. Ice is to frozen liquid as _____ is to strong wind.

24. Teacher is to teach as preacher is to _____.

25. _____ is to 8 sided figure as hexagon is to a 6 sided figure.

26. North America is to Northern Hemisphere as Australia is to _____.

27. _____ is to snow as rake is to leaves.

28. Hammer is to nail as screw driver is to _____.

29. 8 x 3 is to 24 as 12 x _____ is to 24.

30. Digestive system is to stomach as _____ is to lungs.

31. December is to month as _____ is to weight.

Now, create your own phrases and analogies:

1. _____

2. _____

3. _____

4. _____

5. _____

6. _____

7. _____

8. _____

9. _____

10. _____

Cause and Effect

The understanding of **cause and effect** will help your comprehension in reading. You will find clue words in your reading that will indicate cause and effect.

The following are some of the clue words: **so, because, therefore, that was why, as a result, for this reason.**

There are different ways to identify the cause and effect in sentences. Contrary to the traditional method, my favorite way is to find the effect first by asking the question: "What happened in this story on that day?" Then find the cause by asking the question: "Why did it happen?"

Exercise: Find the cause and effect relationships in the following sentences. Draw one line under the <u>effect</u>, and two lines under the <u>cause</u>. Then write the word effect and the word cause correctly above the correct phrase. Circle the clue words for cause and effect in each sentence. (For this activity children could work in groups.)

    cause   *effect*

1. <u>He fell</u> so <u>we all laughed</u>.

2. The radio won't work because the battery is dead.

3. The crowd cheered because he hit a homerun.

4. The hurricane was very strong so the house was blown away.

5. Jane didn't have breakfast this morning so she was very hungry.

6. Allie ran up and down the stairs as a result she was out of breath.

7. He did not study for the test as a result he failed the test.

8. Craig eats like a horse. That is why his mother cooks big meals every day for dinner.

9. She is clumsy as a result she falls easily whenever she walks.

10. Carrie and Frances have never flown in an airplane before so the flight attendant had to fasten their seat belts for them.

11. Michelle was shrunk to about six inches. Therefore her mother had to scale everything in her room to six inches.

12. James damaged his new shoes because he fell in a pond.

13. It started to rain heavily, as a result the crowd ran for cover.

14. People may have cavities because they don't care for their teeth.

15. Billy is wearing a hearing aid, as a result he could hear better.

16. The tire on dad's car is flat because he ran over a long screw.

17. I will be late to get home tonight. For this reason I will probably miss dinner with my great family.

18. The carpet is ruined so my family has to replace it.

19. We heard a crashing sound because a tree had fallen on a house.

20. The telephone was disconnected because the bill was not paid.

21. My family gave me a great present on my birthday so I'm happy.

22. The food in the refrigerator is still fresh therefore we can eat it.

23. My mother is very tall as result she can easily reach the pictures.

24. He accidentally stapled his finger this is why he is bleeding.

25. Frances was in love for this reason she got married to Brandon.

26. It had rained all day as result the basement was flooded.

27. My grandmother got her feet wet because she landed in a swimming pool.

28. Steve and Gary were extremely hungry as a result they ate all the food their mother had cooked that evening.

29. He was grounded because he didn't prepare for the test.

30. The wind blew the antenna off the roof therefore the TV quit.

31. I was grounded by my caring and loving father because I skipped my homework and my chores at home.

32. A fire truck raced down the street because a house is on fire.

33. Jet planes make great noise so people dislike living near airports and highways that lead to airports.

34. Spring is here for this reason, plants are blooming.

35. The water pressure was high so the pipe burst.

36. The sandstorm in the desert is overwhelming therefore the camel's long eyelashes and nostrils protect it from the sand.

37. My bicycle was rusted because it was left under the rain.

38. As a result of the great success the store continued the sale.

39. She had lost her lenses so she could not see very well.

40. The police stopped my teacher because he forgot to pay for the $40 of gas he pumped in his car.

41. The sun is extremely hot today as a result I got some sunburn.

42. I love most people, so most people love me.

Sequencing

Sequencing is the process of putting events in a proper and correct order. In reading, especially for students, the ability to read any material and ordering the events throughout the story should greatly enhance their comprehension skills, and help them to respond appropriately about what is read. There are clue words to help students to correctly order events in a story.

The following are types of clue words that may or may not appear in a story: **first, secondly, next, after, before, then, finally, later, etc.**

Exercise: Use the clue words in sentences to sequence, or put in correct order, all your activities this morning from the time you woke up until the time you arrived at school.

1. first:

_____

2. secondly:

_____

3. then:

_____

4. after:

_____

5. before:

_____

6. later:

_____

7. finally:

_____

Exercise: Read the story below, and sequence, or put the sentences in correct order. Use numbers to correctly order the sentences. #1 will be what happened first, #2 what is next, etc.

The Village King

The village King was the ultimate power in his village. He'd collect taxes, settle arguments, listen to his people's problems, and lock up people who broke the law. In the morning around 7 AM, he'd sit in his hammock. Then he'd slip outside to his porch, where he would speak to the elders about the day's business.

Next, he'd puff out a few smokes from his pipe, grab his cane, and walk around the village to listen to more stories. Finally, after his chores were done, the King would go to bed, after sharing few jokes with his children.

_____The King sat in his hammock.

_____The King was the ultimate power in his village.

_____After his chores were complete he went to bed.

_____He collected taxes and settle arguments.

_____The King shared jokes with his children.

_____He grabbed his cane and walked around the village.

Exercise: Read the story below about how to carve a Halloween pumpkin in six easy steps. On the lines in the pumpkin below, write the sentences correctly in the order in which this is done.

_____ Next, cut a circle around the top of the pumpkin, take off the cap, and clean out the seeds

_____ Finally, put a candle in your jack-o-lantern and display it.

_____ First, choose your pumpkin and your jack-o-lantern pattern.

_____ Then, get a large spoon and a sharp carving knife.

_____ Draw your pattern on the pumpkin.

_____ Cut out the eyes, mouth, nose, and any other parts of the pattern that you need to cut.

1. _____

2. _____

3. _____

4. _____

5. _____

6. _____

Exercise: Use the numbers after the sentences in the story, and order them correctly.

One day, Dustin had a brilliant idea. (5) He dreamed that soon, he would go to a huge lake far away for fishing. He determined that by catching a humongous trout, he would prove his maturity and his skill in fishing. (3) But this was just a distant dream. Justin was only eight years old. But two years later, his grandfather invited him to his farm where there was vast lake with variety of fish. (1) This was the opportunity he had hoped for.

On his third day in the farm, his grandfather decided to take Justin for a fishing trip. (7) To catch a big trout, Justin needed the right hook and line, and a fishing pole. (6) After an hour of fishing, Dustin finally realized his dream. (4) He caught a gargantuan trout that weighed over seven pounds. (2)

1. _____

2. _____

3. _____

4. _____

5. _____

6. _____

7. _____

Exercise: Read the story below. Then number the sentences in the correct order.

There was once a strange house on a hilltop beyond a small populated town. There were eerie, bone-chilling rumors, and horrifying stories that were passed down for generations about this house. Nobody ever saw anyone go in or out of the house. In fact, the townsfolk didn't even know who lived there or owned the place. The house had bright red windows which always stayed locked. The oversized front doors had such huge doorknobs, that any average pair of hands could not grab the knob to open the doors. There was also the persistent fear that whoever visited the house would never come back to the town.

One day, Tom and his friend, Joe, decided to risk an adventurous trip to the house. It was an unspeakable gamble. It took the two of them to turn the knob on the front doors. As they entered the house, a brisk cold air blew in their faces. An old broken-down stairway stood in front of them leading upstairs. There was another narrow dusty stairway, the opening covered with spider webs, leading to the basement. It was this stairway the boys began to descend.

Suddenly three pigeons flew across the boys' heads with such a flapping and squawking that Tom almost fainted. Before they reached the bottom of the basement stairs, they heard some ominous, grunting, spooky sounds. They imagined that a ghost lived down there. But nothing stopped them from exploring the dark, dank basement. All of a sudden, an old man seemed to appear in front of them. He was bent and ragged. His long hair and beard inhabited by spiders and beetles. But he was not a ghost. He was just a homeless man who had made this basement his home.

Now it was up to the boys to decide to carry on the scary traditional stories about the house or to let the townspeople know that the old, dark, spooky house on the hill was no more a mystery, but just a home for the homeless.

_____ Three pigeons flew out of the basement.

_____ A ragged homeless man had made the house his home.

_____ Tom and Joe wanted to explore the house.

_____ The house had bright red windows.

_____ Rumors and fearful stories were passed down in generations.

_____ There was once a strange house on a hilltop.

_____ The mystery about the house was finally solved.

_____ They thought a ghost lived in the house.

_____ Nobody ever visited the house.

Topic Sentences and Supporting Details

A **topic sentence** is a sentence among a group of sentences in a paragraph or in a story that summarizes or tells what a whole story is about. It's the main idea and the star of the story.

The topic sentence may appear at the beginning, in the middle, or at the end of a paragraph, or anywhere in a story.

Example: Ask yourself: "Which one sentence does all the other sentences refer to or explain?" That sentence is the **topic sentence**.

All other sentences would explain and support the topic sentence. They are called <u>supporting details</u>.

Hello, my name is T. S.

The **"T"** stands for **"Topic"** and the **"S"** stands for **"Sentence".** My name is **"Topic Sentence."** I am a star in every story or movie. I'm the main character. Everybody else is important, but can't get anywhere without me. Their name is **"Supporting Details."** They give more information about what my story or movie is about. Name your own stars!

Exercise: Write the topic sentence on the top line, and the details on the next lines.

Topic sentence: _____

Details: _____

Details: _____

Details: _____

Details: _____

Details: _____

Exercise: Read the short stories below. Each story has a topic sentence. Write the topic sentence on the line that follows the story. On the other lines, write the supporting details:

Lions

1. Male lions are the only cats with manes.
2. Hundreds of lions live in captivity in zoos.
3. My class researched to get lots of information about lions.
4. Most people are frightened by the behavior of lions
5. Lions spend about twenty hours a day sleeping or resting.

Topic sentence: _____

Details: _____

Details: _____

Details: _____

Details: _____

The United Nations

1. The United Nations is a world organization established in 1945.
2. It works for world peace, world security, and human prosperity.
3. There are about 166 or more member nations.
4. The General Assembly among the six organs is very important.
5. The Security Council is responsible for keeping the peace.

Topic sentence: _____

Details: _____

Details: _____

Details: _____

Details: _____

Saturday

1. I visit friends and play all kinds of sports.

2. Sometimes we just sit down with snacks and watch movies.

3. The mall is our favorite place to visit.

4. I sleep late because I don't have to go to school that day.

5. Saturday is my favorite day of the week.

6. Saturday is the day before Sunday when I also stay home.

Topic sentence: _____

Details: _____

Details: _____

Details: _____

Details: _____

Details: _____

Plants

1. They produce oxygen which is necessary for all living things.

2. Plants are the engines that support the life of all living things.

3. They use carbon dioxide to prepare their food.

4. They give living things food necessary for energy.

5. They capture the sun's rays to store and create energy.

6. They also reduce the amount of carbon in the atmosphere.

Topic sentence: _____

Details: _____

Details: _____

Details: _____

Details: _____

Details: _____

Bears

1. Bears can move at high speed when they're agitated.

2. They'll attack anything that threatens them.

3. They have very short tempers and get easily angry.

4. They are known to attack and kill humans.

5. Bears can be very dangerous animals especially those with cubs.

Topic sentence: _____

Details: _____

Details: _____

Details: _____

Details: _____

Dancing

1. My sister and I just learned how to do the hustle.

2. My mom loves to do the twist.

3. All my friends do the electric slide.

4. My grandmother used to do the jitterbug.

5. There are many new dances that will ever come and go.

6. I wonder what kind of dance will come next.

Topic sentence: _____

Details: _____

Details: _____

Details: _____

Details: _____

Details: _____

Food

1. Food is a necessary element for the existence of all living things.

2. Food helps us to grow and survive.

3. Without it we'll die.

4. It gives us the energy we need to work and play.

5. Food also keeps us healthy.

Topic sentence: _____

Details: _____

Details: _____

Details: _____

Details: _____

Newspapers

1. They give us local and world news.

2. They feature news, sports, weather, ads, obituaries, etc.

3. Newspapers are very useful and can be used for many things.

4. They are also useful for classroom teaching.

Topic sentence: _____

Details: _____

Details: _____

Details: _____

Exercise: Research and write detailed sentences for the following topic sentences. Remember to write about at least the five most important supporting details about the topic sentence:

My Favorite Summer

Topic sentence: _____

Details: _____

Details: _____

Details: _____

Details: _____

Details: _____

Shakespeare, World Famous Author

Topic sentence: _____

Details: _____

Details: _____

Details: _____

Details: _____

Details: _____

Egypt and the River Nile

Topic sentence: _____

Details: _____

Details: _____

Details: _____

Details: _____

Details: _____

Abbreviations

An **abbreviation** is a way to shorten a word. Some words can either be proper or common nouns. A capital letter is used when abbreviating for Proper Nouns.

A period is used at the end of all abbreviations.

Example: captain --- Capt.; ounce --- oz.; mister --- Mr.

Street --- St. or street --- st.

Exercise: Write the abbreviation for the following words:

1. mister _____   2. doctor _____

3. street _____   4. December _____

5. post office _____   6. Monday _____

7. company _____   8. road _____

9. governor _____   10. Indiana _____

11. senator _____   12. president _____

13. junior _____   14. Florida _____

15. lieutenant _____   16. April _____

17. Missus _____   18. Ohio _____

19. department _____   20. et cetera _____

21. mountain   _____

22. example   _____

23. Tuesday   _____

24. Nebraska   _____

25. July   _____

26. miss   _____

27. registered nurse _____

28. Sunday   _____

29. United Nations _____

30. railroad   _____

31. boulevard   _____

32. parkway   _____

33. Wednesday _____

Abbreviations for Measurement

Exercise: Write the abbreviations for the measurements on the line on the right:

1. inch _____

2. foot _____

3. yard _____

4. mile _____

5. pint _____

6. quart _____

7. gallon _____

8. ounce _____

9. pound _____

10. millimeter _____

11. centimeter _____

12. meter _____

13. decimeter _____

14. kilometer _____

15. liter _____

16. gram _____

17. feet _____

18. quarts _____

Contractions/Apostrophe

A **contraction** is a shortened version of a word created from two words. An **apostrophe** is used to show where one or more letters are left out when the two words are combined.

Exercise: Write the contractions opposite to the words in the parentheses and use each contraction in a good sentence.

1. (let us)   _____   1. _____

2. (will not)   _____   2. _____

3. (I am)   _____   3. _____

4. (we are)   _____   4. _____

5. (he is)   _____   5. _____

6. (should not)   _____   6. _____

7. (they are)   _____   7. _____

8. (can not)   _____   8. _____

9. (would not)   _____   9. _____

10. (must not)   _____   10. _____

11. (are not)   _____   11. _____

12. (she is)   _____   12. _____

13. (you are) _____ 13. _____

14. (is not) _____ 14. _____

15. (they would) _____ 15. _____

16. (was not) _____ 16. _____

17. (I have) _____ 17. _____

18. (there is) _____ 18. _____

19. (we would) _____ 19. _____

20. (who is) _____ 20. _____

21. (has not) _____ 21. _____

22. (were not) _____ 22. _____

23. (had not) _____ 23. _____

24. (it will) _____ 24. _____

25. (does not) _____ 25. _____

26. (we have) _____ 26. _____

27. (he is) _____ 27. _____

28. (did not) _____ 28. _____

29. (I would) _____ 29. _____

Generalizing-Clue Words

A **generalization** is a special way of drawing conclusions. It is a broad statement based on facts. A generalization that is based on more than one or two facts usually has a good chance of being valid. An invalid statement is one which is not true or cannot be true. There are however some exceptions.

Clue words for generalizing include all, many, any, almost, few, most, anyone, none, always, never, several, no, every, only, everybody, some, generally, nearly, etc.

Exercise: Read each sentence below, circle the 'generalizing' clue word, and write *valid* if the generalization can be true and *invalid* if it is not or cannot be true.

1. All birds can fly for long distances. _____

2. Some jungle plants are used by doctors to make medicines. _____

3. Most students who really work hard in school get good grades. _____

4. Everyone agrees that all bad weather is caused by climate change. _____

5. Many people keep snakes and parakeets as pets. _____

6. Everybody believes that an asteroid will hit Earth some day. _____

7. My teacher never smiles to her students. _____

8. I have some friends who never have gone for fishing. _____

9. My sister says that yellow is everyone's favorite color. _____

10. To be healthy, it's necessary to eat all balanced foods. _____

11. Several adults have never gone to Washington D. C. _____

12. In my classroom, everybody is a great singer. _____

13. Many adults like to watch football on television. _____

14. None of the girls can ever be in cheerleading. _____

15. Any grown-up can lift a 100-pound rock. _____

16. I believe that most ford cars are reliable. _____

17. It is never warm in the fall. _____

18. Nobody knows what the weather will be tomorrow. _____

19. All warm-blooded creatures live in a jungle. _____

20. Some people prefer to take vacations in the summer. _____

21. Only birds have feathers. _____

22. It is always good for the body to have enough sleep. _____

23. Almost every day brings its own challenges. _____

24. Only people with long legs should do the high jump. _____

25. Cats and dogs are always enemies. _____

26. Almost all the students in grade four hate to eat spinach. _____

27. Generally, many products we use today come from China. _____

28. All modern inventions come from Asia. _____

29. Nearly everyone today uses paper in some way. _____

30. Every food product in our grocery stores is wrapped in paper. _____

31. No storms are followed by a large rainbow. _____

32. Some English words come from old English. _____

33. Few pine trees survive in the winter weather. _____

34. No one can lift that 100 pound bag of rocks. _____

35. Many fantastic and successful writers read a great deal. _____

36. All children love cats for pets. _____

37. Most movie shows last only for half an hour. _____

38. All carnivores eat humans for food. _____

39. Nearly all of Africa is covered by forests. _____

40. Several people in the audience admired him. _____

41. None of us will ever be able to use the computer. _____

42. Only tall and muscular people are fit to play basketball. _____

43. Some people believe that UFO's do exist. _____

44. Few of my friends agree with my odd & strange opinion. _____

45. Some people who join a fitness club are there to lose weight. _____

46. Most students love to stay home on snow-days. _____

47. Homework is always necessary to make good grades. _____

48. Several students love to listen to music during homework. _____

49. I love all kinds of music. How about you? _____

50. His awards were all about nothing. _____

51. None of the basketball players appreciated the game. _____

52. Do we all enjoy the picnic today? _____

53. My friends think that all our restaurants serve diet food. _____

54. All the street signs are correct and are there for motorists. _____

55. My teacher is always right in my opinion. _____

Compare and Contrast - Clue Words

By **comparing and contrasting** figures, ideas, pictures, etc. we learn to understand how two or more things are different and also how they are similar.

Comparison states what two or more things have in common or their similarities. **Contrast** states how two or more things are different.

They both help us to organize our thoughts and understand information.

Exercise: Look at the picture of a lion and a giraffe and complete the assignment.

Lion

Giraffe

Compare: How are a lion and a giraffe alike?

1. _____

2. _____

3. _____

4. _____

5. _____

Contrast: How are a lion and a giraffe different?

6. _____

7. _____

8. _____

9. _____

10. _____

Exercise: Use your statements above and write a paragraph comparing and contrasting the lion and the giraffe.

_____

_____

_____

_____

_____

_____

_____

_____

_____

_____

_____

_____

_____

_____

_____

Comparison states what two things have in common. It points out the similarities between two things.

Comparison clue words include the following: **like, as, also, too, similarly, in comparison.** Most of the time, although not always, the clue words will help you to determine whether you are comparing or contrasting.

Exercise: Read each sentence, underline the clue word, and circle the two things that are compared.

1. Mary is a two-faced monster, and her sister Joan is too.

2. My mother is as wise as an owl.

3. The planet Saturn has rings. Similarly, Uranus has rings.

4. A hurricane is a strong wind. A tornado is too.

5. Mike is a one-legged cowboy. His brother is like him also.

6. In comparison to his brother Andy, Chad is a fast runner.

7. Lions are members of the cat family. Tigers are also.

8. Her father is very tall, and her mother is too.

9. My uncle is always as hungry as an elephant.

10. Alex's freckles are like spotted dots on his face.

11. The room was as hot as it is in the tropics.

12. In comparison to his wife, Mike has cross eyes.

13. She is as furious as a worm on fish hook.

Contrast states how two things are different. It brings out what is not common about two things. **Contrast clue words** include the following: **unlike, but, however, though, although, nevertheless, on the other hand, in contrast.**

Most of the time, although not always, the clue words will help you determine whether you are contrasting or comparing.

Exercise: Read each sentence below, underline the clue word and circle the two things that are contrasted.

1. His uncle is short, though his aunt is very tall.

2. My sister plays baseball, but my brother plays football.

3. The North American bees are gentle insects. However, the African bees are very aggressive and can kill humans.

4. Math is my favorite subject in school. My sister on the other hand likes reading.

5. My family likes spinach on the dinner table, nevertheless, I always prefer to eat fruits.

6. Although the African cobra is considered to be very poisonous, the mamba is even more poisonous.

7. Sister Frances likes pizza, but my younger brother likes burgers.

8. Though I love to read books, John loves to watch television.

9. Unlike the Mississippi River which flows south, the Nile River flows north.

10. Andy's family enjoys the Christmas season at home. On the other hand, John's family prefers to vacation in Hawaii.

11. James is a hard-working student in school. In contrast, his friend is smart but lazy.

12. Mercury takes a shorter time to revolve around the sun. Nevertheless, Pluto takes a longer time to do so.

13, My computer is still printing, even though it has no ink.

14. Transportation in other countries is really poor. In contrast transportation in America is very advanced.

15. A helicopter can only carry few people. However, a jumbo jet can transport hundreds of people at the same time

Prefixes and Suffixes

A **prefix** is one or more letters or syllables added to the beginning of a root word to change its meaning.

A **suffix** is one or more letters or syllables added at the end of a root word to change its meaning.

Most of the prefixes and suffixes have meanings.

Exercise: Read each word below, under the correct column, put the part that's the prefix under prefix, the root word under root word, and the suffix under suffix. Note: some words have two suffixes.

WORD	ROOT WORD	PREFIX	SUFFIX
1. unhurt	_____	_____	_____
2. disagreement	_____	_____	_____
3. powerless	_____	_____	_____
4. unfriendly	_____	_____	_____
5. inaccurately	_____	_____	_____
6. creator	_____	_____	_____
7. unselfish	_____	_____	_____
8. misunderstand	_____	_____	_____

WORD	ROOT WORD	PREFIX	SUFFIX
9. displeased	_____	_____	_____
10. nonstop	_____	_____	_____
11. thoughtfulness	_____	_____	_____
12. cars	_____	_____	_____
13. washable	_____	_____	_____
14. neighborhood	_____	_____	_____
15. usefulness	_____	_____	_____
16. indigestion	_____	_____	_____
17. teacher	_____	_____	_____
18. foolishness	_____	_____	_____
19. terrorism	_____	_____	_____
20. immature	_____	_____	_____
21. discouraged	_____	_____	_____
22. impossible	_____	_____	_____
23. misplaced	_____	_____	_____

Synonyms

Synonyms are two words that can be interchanged in a context and are said to be 'synonymous relative to the context'.

Example: I saw the big star. --- I saw the large star.

Exercise: Rewrite the story below and use an appropriate synonym generated from brainstorming with your class to substitute or replace the word 'big' wherever it appears in the story. You may use the synonyms in boldface below only after your brainstorming with partners in a group.

There was once a big white house on a big, isolated hill beyond a small town. The big house had big bright red windows which always stayed closed. The big dusty front door had a big doorknob. No one had visited the big house in a very long time. There were rumors and a big fear that whoever visited the big house was never seen again, and never returned to the town.

One day, Tom and his friend Joe, decided to risk a big adventurous trip to explore the big house. As they entered the house, they saw a big old broken-down stairway leading upstairs and another doorway leading down to a big basement. It was this stairway that they chose to descend.

While exploring the big basement, they heard big loud bone-chilling noises. They ran back up the big staircase to get away from the frightful noises.

When they entered a big room on the first floor, they discovered that the big racket they'd heard did not come from ghosts. A big man seemed to suddenly appear before them. It was just a homeless man who had made the big house his home. What a big relief for Tom and Joe!

Now it was up to the boys to decide to carry on the big, scary, traditional stories about the <u>big</u> house or to let the townspeople know that the <u>big</u>, old, dark, spooky house on the hill was no more a <u>big</u> mystery, but just a home for the homeless.

List of possible synonyms for big to use:
bombastic, colossal, considerable, cumbersome, deep, enormous, elephantine, full size, gargantuan, giant, gigantic, great, huge, humongous, husky, immense, large, life size, lofty, magnanimous, mammoth, massive, roomy, significant, sizable, spacious, titanic, towering, vast

Exercise: Write your own story using the synonyms above or find more on your own. Remember that the story should have the writing rubrics requirement.

_____

_____

_____

_____

_____

_____

_____

_____

_____

_____

_____

_____

_____

_____

_____

_____

_____

_____

Exercise: Rewrite the story about Abraham Lincoln and use an appropriate synonym to substitute or replace the word 'great' or 'greatest' wherever they appear in the story. You may use the synonyms in boldface below.

Abraham Lincoln was truly a <u>great</u> president. Some people think he was the <u>greatest</u> president this country ever had. He held this <u>great</u> country together during the Civil War. The Gettysburg Address is still regarded as the <u>greatest</u> speech ever given by an American president. However, not every citizen saw Lincoln as a <u>great</u> hero. Then again, most people felt he was a man of <u>great</u> honesty and vision. His nickname "Honest Abe" came about because of his <u>great</u> character. His death was a <u>great</u> tragedy and loss for the American people.

Synonyms for great may be:
amazing, awesome, celebrated, distinguished, eminent, excellent, fabulous, famous, fantastic, grand, illustrious, impressive, magnificent, notable, outstanding, profound, remarkable, skillful, stately, stupendous, superb, super, talented, terrific, tremendous, wonderful

Exercise: Use the synonyms above and yours and write a story about any topic. Remember that your story should

- stay on topic,
- uses complete and varied ideas,
- has a beginning, middle, and an ending,
- does not ramble or repeat,
- uses strong verbs, and
- good sentence patterns.

_____

_____

_____

_____

_____

_____

_____

_____

_____

_____

_____

_____

_____

_____

Exercise: Read the story below and copy the words in boldface on a piece of paper. Then write an appropriate synonym for each word without losing the meaning of the story. Work in a group or with a partner.

Chester was a **little** field mouse. His **first** day at the river bank was the **beginning** of a most **unusual life experience** for a mouse. He saw a **large cuplike** leaf lying **against** the **shore**. He **carefully stepped** into it. And the next thing he knew, he was **floating** away from the shore in his **newly found** boat. Now, a **strong** wind had blown his boat out into the **middle** of the river.

The mouse **didn't know how** to **search** for food, **hide** from his **enemies**, or find **shelter** from the wind and water. Worst of all, he was not aware of the **unseen danger** that was **all around** him. A **huge** white gull had **spied** him from **high above**.

Soon, Chester heard a **whole multitude** of gulls **screaming** through the air. They **settled down** on the water and **paddled** up **alongside** the little boat. Chester felt like he was in **really big trouble**!

What he didn't **realize** was that a **school of fish** was **close by** and **one of them** had seen the gulls. The fish **surfaced** and were just **waiting** for the gulls to **tip over** the **little** boat. They **planned** to **snap up** the little mouse. What he **didn't see** was **further above** him.

Just then, a **huge** fish hawk **appeared** over the boat, the mouse, the gulls, and the fish. The hawk **swiftly swooped down** with his **powerful** wings. With the **tip** of one of his wings, he **brushed** the edge of the boat and **tipped it over**.

When the hawk **flew off**, he had the fish in his **beak**. His **presence scattered** the gulls. But Chester was **lost** in the water. He **sank down** under the water, and then came up **sputtering**. **Instinctively** he **began** to swim. **Paddling furiously**, he swam **towards** his little boat. He was **hanging onto** the side of the leaf, but the boat was **pushed** by the **current** into some rocks. Then it was **flung** upon the **sandy shore**.

Chester **jumped** off the leaf, and **leaped** for the bushes **avoiding** the **waiting** gulls who **returned** to the water. He was **soaking wet** and **hungry**. To **find** food, he would have **to leave** his **hiding place** beneath the bushes. So **as long as** he could **hear** the **screams** of the gulls, he **stayed safe**, but **miserable**, beneath the brush. In a **short while** everything became **quiet**.

Finally, Chester **crept cautiously** into **the open**. **Growing bolder**, he began to **roll** in the grass. He could only **hear** the **faint rustling** and **murmurs** of air through the **brush and grass**. And in the moonlight, Chester **realized** he was **alone**. His **enemies** were **gone**.

Knowing your synonyms: A synonym is a word or words that mean the same as another word and can be used as such in your writing.

Example: The synonyms for 'dirty' can be filthy, unclean, messy, etc.

Exercise: On the line by each word, write a synonym for that word.

WORD BOX

jubilant	robust	unhappy	thin	sure	spooky	tidy
witty	great	noisy	humongous	hole	error	nice
brilliant	rich	brave	annoying	slender	oversize	husky
clean	splendid	wise	begin	creepy	whispered	fix
Jubilant	murmured	brave	titanic	fast	amazing	duty
trot	abundant	attractive	untrue	begin	father	edible
whispered	jubilant	amusing	brave	sad	wise	titanic
hole	collect	wonderful	tiny	small	soak	scary
beautiful	bright	intelligent	abundant	huge	plenty	

1. rich _____

2. gifted _____

3. tidy _____

4. fearless _____

5. intelligent _____

6. error _____

7. small _____

8. aggravating _____

9. dad _____

10. vacant _____

11. quick _____

12. miserable _____

13. certain _____

14. hilarious _____

15. sad _____

16. boisterous _____

17. eerie _____

18. monstrous _____

19. false _____

20. outstanding _____

21. slender _____

22. delicious _____

23. clean _____

24. gather _____

25. shiny _____

26. repair _____

27. yell _____

28. work _____

29. start _____

30. slim _____

31. jumbo _____

32. wonderful _____

33. many _____

34. splendid _____

35. creepy _____

36. gorgeous _____

37. oversized _____

38. exceptional _____

39. fat _____   40. microscopic _____

41. gap _____   42. depressed _____

43. galloped _____   44. murmured _____

45. wet _____   46. gargantuan _____

47. comical _____   48. marvelous _____

49. joyful _____   50. brilliant _____

51. chuckled _____   52. knowledge _____

53. attractive _____   54. terrified _____

Exercise: B

Circle the synonym or the phrase that means the same or almost the same as the word in boldface:

1. massive **appetite**:

   A. thirsty   B. hungry   C. disappointed   D. surprised

2. **similar** situation:

   A. different   B. same   C. difficult   D. long

3. **delicious** food:

   A. sour   B. cooked   C. balanced   D. tasty

4. **prompt** action:

   A. delayed   B. slow   C. quick   D. meaningful

5. **legal** affair:

A. inform   B. pleasant   C. humorous   D. lawful

6. television **interview**:

A. questions   B. preview   C. show   D. movie

7. **massive** earthquake:

A. loud   B. immense   C. magma   D. destructive

8. **achieved** goal:

A. huge   B. fulfilled   C. unpleasant   D. forgotten

9. **honest** misunderstanding:

A. gloomy   B. clear   C. upright   D. confusion

10. an **eerie** graveyard:

A. dark   B. abandoned   C. quiet   D. spooky

11. state **boundary**:

A. limit   B. governor   C. legislator   D. map

12. **aching** back:

A. broad   B. powerful   C. injured   D. painful

13. parent **support**:

A. traveling   B. dependent   C. assistance   D. love

14. an **uneven** time:

A. pleasurable   B. unequal   C. late   D. forgettable

15. **risky** business:

A. junk   B. good   C. incomplete   D. dangerous

16. **gigantic** mountain:

A. tall   B. rocky   C. humongous   D. range

17. **witty** statement:

    A. hilarious   B. incorrect   C. true   D. disappointing

18. **nervous** moment:

    A. anxious   B. calm   C. relaxed   D. time

19. **ultimate** sacrifice:

    A. lowest   B. worst   C. doubtful   D. highest

20. **respectful** student:

    A. bright   B. polite   C. famous   D. quiet

Antonyms

Antonyms are two words that express opposing concepts. The opposite of synonyms.

Example: hot --- cold; inside --- outside; comfort ---discomfort

Exercise: Circle the antonym or the phrase that is opposite or almost opposite to the word in boldface:

1. **a depressed and gloomy** day:
   A. sorry   B. bright   C. happy   D. damp

2. a large **purchase**:
   A. own   B. store   C. sale   D. freedom

3. **seldom** seen event:
   A. often   B. enjoyable   C. huge   D. anticipated

4. an **invisible** germ:
   A. small   B. seen   C. dangerous   D. lively

5. a **frail** patient:
   A. strong   B. loving   C. waitress   D. dog

6. her **sincere** opinion:
   A. real   B. true   C. phony   D. clear

7. **near to** the road:
   A. close to   B. far from   C. end of   D. long way

8. a **wasted** time:

  A. righted   B. o'clock   C. minutes   D. saved

9. his **uncertain** future:

  A. sure   B. doubtful   C. common   D. great

10. a **voluntary** gesture:

  A. favorable   B. forced   C. quick   D. honest

11. an **unreliable** person:

  A. dependable   B. friendly   C. dangerous   D. strange

12. the **harmless** creature:

  A. dangerous   B. normal   C. bizarre   D. risky

13. the **backward** tribe:

  A. lonely   B. remote   C. forward   D. civilized

14. an **unknown** record:

  A. scarce   B. recognized   C. false   D. split

15. a **peculiar** incident:

  A. great   B. pleasant   C. normal   D. often

16. a **decreased** amount:

  A. expanded   B. lowered   C. final   D. accurate

17. **ancient** times:

  A. old   B. separate   C. modern   D. happy

18. **similar** problems:

  A. mismatched   B. aged   C. difficult   D. serious

19. his **deceased** parent:

  A. alive   B. dead   C. kind   D. beautiful

20. **current** news:

    A. good   B. old   C. television   D. bad

21. the **sturdy** table:

    A. large   B. crowded   C. tall   D. weak

22. an **experienced** worker:

    A. unskilled   B. serious   C. effective   D. huge

Homonyms

Homonyms are words which sound exactly alike but are not spelled the same and do not mean the same thing.

    Example: eight --- ate; right --- write

Exercise: Write a homonym opposite each word on the line below:

1. hole   _____   2. pale   _____

3. weight   _____   4. flour   _____

5. reed   _____   6. sum   _____

7. through   _____   8. by   _____

9. stare   _____   10. blue   _____

11. rode   _____   12. bear   _____

13. bee   _____   14. lead   _____

15. new   _____   16. male   _____

17. night   _____   18. fair   _____

19. steal   _____   20. tail   _____

21. peace   _____   22. sail   _____

23. mist   _____   24. bee   _____

25. scene   _____   26. dye   _____

27. plane _____   28. too _____

29. pane _____   30. whether _____

31. sore _____   32. sun _____

33. cellar _____   34. waste _____

35. seams _____   36. write _____

37. due _____   38. dear _____

39. toe _____   40. sea _____

41. weak _____   42. cent _____

43. meat _____   44. know _____

45. weigh _____   46. their _____

Exercises:

1. Write a paragraph using fifteen of the homonyms that are listed above.

2. Write a poem and use as many homonyms from this list as you can.

_____

_____

_____

_____

_____

_____

_____

4 Categorizing

Categorizing is the practice of **classifying**, **organizing**, and **grouping** your *thoughts, events, characters, and ideas* in what you read. This process should enhance and improve your comprehension.

Categorizing should help you to **process**, **understand**, and **remember information** much better. The exercises below should assist you to practice this skill.

Exercise: Match the list of words on your left of the page with the category list on the right. Write the correct letter by the word.

Words

1. cowboy _____
2. farmhouse _____
3. whisper _____
4. sweater _____
5. soccer _____
6. ditch _____

Category

a. happy
b. large things
c. reptile
d. circus
e. sad word
f. dwelling

7. humongous   _____   g. cooking ways

8. tumbler   _____   h. hole

9. baking   _____   i. boat word

10. cruise   _____   j. sport

11. sharks   _____   k. likes water

12. dreary   _____   l. family

13. decrease   _____   m. quantity, number

14. nocturnal   _____   n. winter fun

15. grandparents   _____   o. night event

16. sleigh   _____   p. quiet sound

17. rustling   _____   q. very small

18. minuscule   _____   r. rodeo

19. snake   _____   s. clothing

Exercise: Assign a category to each list of words below:

1. _____

      picnic

      swimming

      vacation

      traveling

      camping

2. _____

      joyful

      cheerful

      amusing

      enjoyable

      pleasing

3. _____

      spinach

      lettuce

      potato

      carrots

      greens

4. _____

      flamingos

      parakeets

      geese

      pigeons

      hawks

5. _____

    diamonds

    iron

    rocks

    metal

    enamel

6. _____

    square

    pentagon

    round

    rectangular

    cylinder

7. _____

    bang

    siren

    loudspeaker

    microphone

    scream

8. _____

    asteroid

    Milky Way

    Space Shuttle

    meteors

    comets

9. _____

    blade

    needles

    thumbtack

    edge

    nail

10. _____

    pencils

    scissors

    rulers

    paper

    crayons

11. _____

    oranges

    bananas

    grapes

    watermelon

    kiwis

12. _____

    saucepan

    oven

    dishwasher

    refrigerator

    cabinets

Exercise: Read the list of words below, make a correct category title for each list, and put the words under that category title that you choose:

Words:

microscopic	upset	soil	Mathematics
small	kites	petite	gargantuan
agitate	heart	earth	torment
sod	little	dirt	physical education
wings	helicopter	huge	music
vex	minuscule	gigantic	rocks
space shuttle	oversize	English	digestive system
neck	disturb	kidney	airplane
immense	humongous	balloons	esophagus
mountains	Science	midget	bother

Category:	Category:	Category:

Category:	Category:	Category:

Category:	Category:	Category:

Idioms

Idioms are figures of expression in which there are always a deeper meaning beneath what the words appear to be saying. They may say one thing but mean another. Authors use idioms to give more meaning, to 'spice up', or to add more suspense to their story.

Example: My teacher <u>lost her cool</u> when I hit that kid in my class.

The idiom: 'lost her cool' simply means that she was angry.

You are in hot water.

The idiom 'hot water' means you are in big trouble.

Exercise: Match the idioms on this page with their meanings by using the letters on the next page:

1. My mother always says that I'm walking on thin ice when I don't behave.

   _____

2. My little sister gets on my nerve every day for messing with my toys.

   _____

3. Her eyes popped out when the secret was finally revealed to our family.

   _____

4. Please don't cut in when I'm speaking to your mother.

   _____

5. The old man kicked the bucket at the age of ninety-two.

   _____

6. Some people just get blue in the face when they are really, really angry.

   _____

7. The teams wanted to see each other face to face during their debate.

   _____

8. He's really a cool guy.

   _____

9. "You are on a slippery slope for your bad choices!" my mom screamed.

   _____

10. Friends usually bury the hatchet after a little disagreement.

    _____

11. The rowdy crowd was told to get lost if they didn't behave.

    _____

12. When the wind died down, we went outside to continue the game.

    _____

13. She might lose her job if she continues to make waves.

    _____

14. The football game was cancelled because it was raining cats and dogs.

    _____

15. I bit off more than I could chew when I accepted this project.

    _____

16. Dad said that I already had two strikes against me for getting into trouble.

    _____

17. "Knock it off!" my coach demanded as we argued with the other players.

_____

18. Sometimes you need to hold your tongue when others are speaking.

_____

19. I have reached the end of my rope.

_____

20. He always blows his stack when others disagrees with him.

_____

21. "You should tow the line," the principal told her students.

_____

22. We all hit the deck as the tornado blew over us.

_____

23. Give a big hand to our illustrious speaker.

_____

24. Please make room for the crowd of people that are still arriving.

_____

25. It's not my bag to make friends with that type of people.

_____

26. Students who go off the deep end with their work usually get bad grades.

_____

27. It's like looking for a needle in a haystack.

_____

28. I want you to be busy around the clock as long as you work here.

    _____

29. You just hit the nail right on the head.

    _____

30. Some people miss the boat when they fail to take advantage of an opportunity like this.

    _____

31. I saw the handwriting on the wall before it ever occurred.

    _____

32. Please drop me a line when you arrive in Paris.

    _____

33. Hold your horses when you're in line at the bank or waiting for the cashier.

    _____

34. Our dad will blow his top if we don't tell the truth.

    _____

Meanings of idioms to be matched with their expressions:

a. angry   b. died

c. disappear   d. hurry up

e. nice person   f. almost in big trouble

g. angry   h. interrupt

i. keep quiet and still   j. stop, cease

k. agree   l. create more space

m. make peace, forgive

n. make nervous, upset

o. surprised

p. create a disturbance

q. have one more chance

r. more work than I can manage

s. not what I like to do

t. obey authority

u. pushed to the limit

v. applaud by clapping

w. decreased/ slowed

x. become very angry

y. in a haste/hurry/rush

z. hit the floor

aa. be patient

bb. hard to find

cc. write me a letter

dd. missed an opportunity

ee. got it right

ff. angry

5 Similes and Metaphors

A **simile** is a figure of speech in which a person, a place, an object, a feeling, or an idea is compared to something else to show how they are alike by using the words 'like' and 'as'.

Example: He runs as fast as a hare.

My other friend walks like a snail.

A **metaphor** also compares people, places, things, feelings, and ideas *without* using the connecting words 'like' and 'as'.

Example: My mother is a very beautiful flower.

My tongue is a firing hot volcano when I taste a hot food.

Exercise: On the line after each sentence, write 'simile' if the sentence is a simile, and the word 'metaphor' if the sentence is a metaphor, and underline the two things being compared.

1. The funnel cloud is as dark as charcoal.

_____

2. She is as stubborn as a mule.

_____

3. My hair was an entangled rope before I went to the hair salon.

_____

4. The General's orders were as clear as mud.

_____

5. My sister can swim like a fish.

_____

6. The long fireman's water hose was a long South African anaconda.

_____

7. The famous athlete runs like an African gazelle.

_____

8. She was so happy for the Christmas gift that her face gleamed like the moon.

_____

9. The hot kitchen was a heated oven.

_____

10. The hardworking construction manager is as busy as a bee.

_____

11. I was as proud as a peacock when my sister won the prize.

_____

12. The hazy figure in the fog was as scary as a giant ghost.

_____

13. Her smile was a contagious boost to the whole family.

_____

14. His hopes disappeared like a dream when he didn't finish the race.

_____

15. That hot chili is a dangerous volcano.

_____

16. The northern star is as bright as a street light.

_____

17. The lion's roar is a huge scare for everyone in the village.

_____

18. Our neighborhood is as quiet as an abandoned graveyard.

_____

19. The speaker is a great inspiration when he speaks.

_____

20. Her sweet voice is like honey.

_____

21. My little sister is always a hungry elephant.

_____

22. Mrs. Jones is an angel in disguise.

_____

23. My grandparents are as wise as owls.

_____

24. When dad gets home from work, he's a tired lion.

_____

25. She looks like a queen when she dresses for parties.

_____

26. My mouth is as dry as the Sahara Desert when I'm thirsty.

_____

27. The construction worker is a busy bee.

_____

28. When John runs, he's a fast running cheetah.

_____

29. My sister's hair is like a bird's nest.

_____

30. The water is as cold as ice.

_____

31. His aunt is a sweet honey bee.

_____

32. The street light is as bright as a burning star.

_____

33. The Olympic athlete swims like a shark.

_____

34. It is as squirmy as a desperate worm on a fish hook.

_____

35. The candy is as hard as a rock.

_____

36. My silver coin is like a shiny full moon in the clear night's sky.

_____

Hyperbole

Hyperbole is a figure of speech where an extravagant exaggeration is used in one's writing to emphasize a point or meaning.

Example: Her fingernails were so long that they could reach from the United States to India.

Exercise: Can you create your own hyberboles? Give it a try!

_____

_____

_____

_____

_____

_____

_____

_____

_____

_____

Personification

Using **personification**, another figure of speech, in your writing allows you to attribute human traits to inanimate objects.

Personification takes place when emotions, desires, sensations, physical gestures and speech are stated in context of non-living things. This figure of speech may be one of the most effective tools one uses in one's writing. It allows the writer to create a more clear picture in the reader's mind and helps the reader to relate to the object.

> Example: Fear knocked on the door and she answered it.
>
> The camera loves me.
>
> The computer hates me.
>
> The moon smiled at us.

Exercise: Use your imagination and create sentences using personification.

_____

_____

_____

_____

_____

_____

_____

_____

Alliteration

Another figure of speech used often in literature and poetry is **alliteration**. This is the use of the same consonant at the beginning of each stressed syllable in a line of verse. It can also be the repetition of the same sounds or of the same kind of sounds at the beginning of words. An author can also alliterate using vowel sounds.

Example: *mall madness*

sudden sunshine sneaking and surrounding a stunning day

women working their way within winding walls

saturday symphony of sound and scent

traders traveling trekking trendy trifles

boys bustling busily browsing

girls giggling gustily grabbing

chattering like chipmunks chewing chopped nuts

shopkeepers showing shoppers shiny shells from the shore

men minding manners, mixing and matching

teens taking turns telling tales, teasing together

children chiding and chillin' with chums chatting

parents paying for packages to post posthaste

staying till stars stain the stark sky

a melee of mall madness, a mecca of moods

(with permission of the authors, from <u>Musings with Mary and Michael</u>)

Exercise: Can you write a short verse using alliteration?

_____

_____

_____

_____

_____

_____

Exercise: Write the type of figure of speech each sentence demonstrates.

alliteration   personification   idiom

simile   metaphor   hyperbole

1. The trees in the jungle whispered gently in my ears. _____

2. My father roars like a lion when he's really angry. _____

3. Put his foot in his mouth. _____

4. She is as sly as a fox. _____

5. My mother's dress is a rainbow of different colors. _____

6. He is so strong, he can hold the world with one hand. _____

7. The tornado moved over the town like a speeding bullet. _____

8. My brilliant friend can think like a computer. _____

9. Friendly famous Freddy flatly forgot future friends. _____

10. My teacher told me to 'knock it off'. _____

11. Her appetite was so huge that she could eat an elephant. _____

12. The stars tickled me when they twinkled. _____

13. Curious Casey considers Count Caplan courageous. _____

14. My ninety-two year old grandfather is as wise as an owl. _____

15. His heart is like a granite stone. _____

16. Rugged Rachel runs rough rigorous races. _____

17. Her pet dog weighs a ton. _____

18. He kicked the bucket at age ninety-two after a long illness. _____

19. She is so hungry, she can eat an elephant. _____

20. My baby sister's skin is like a smooth soft silk. _____

21. Peter privately places pleasant pets personally. _____

22. Please don't 'fool around' with your science project. _____

23. His excitement can shoot him to the moon. _____

24. The broken computer is whispering for repair. _____

25. The roses in the garden are dancing in the wind. _____

26. The naughty boy was commanded to 'get lost'. _____

27. My hands are as rough as a crocodile skin. _____

28. My uncle's old car devours a large amount of gasoline. _____

29. Ordinary organizers often operate openly. _____

30. The sun winked at me with a gentle 'good morning'. _____

31. Her sharp large eyes can see hundred miles away. _____

32. The crowd was as quiet as a graveyard atmosphere. _____

33. John is a hungry ravenous lion when he eats. _____

34. She said Sam Stanley sings some serious sober serenade songs. _____

35. Mary's old painful knees are complaining about serious aches. _____

36. It was raining 'cats and dogs' yesterday. _____

37. Soft white clouds hung over the sky like cotton. _____

38. She snores as loud as a passing freight train. _____

39. Any superman can jump over Mt. Everest. _____

40. The lonely deer begged the hunter to spare his life. _____

41. The theater is so huge that the whole world could squeeze in it. _____

42. Different daffodils disappear during dangerous droughts. _____

6 Types of Literature

There are many types of literature. Here are some definitions of many types of literature.

Biography: a story of a person's life written by someone else

Autobiography: a biography written by a person about his or her own life

Fiction: a non-factual story with imaginary characters and events

Non Fiction: is a factual story with real characters and events

Historical Fiction: an imaginary story about a historical event or a person in history

Fairy tales: an interesting but highly unlikely story

Fables: a short story that teaches a moral or lesson, often with animal characters

Legend: a story about mythical or supernatural beings or events describing incidents of long ago or how they came to be

Myth: a traditional story accepted as history, expresses the beliefs or the world view of a group of people

Folktales: a tale circulated by word of mouth among the common folk; a story that is about the beliefs, customs and traditions of a group of people passed down generation to generation

Fantasy: imagination (fiction) unrestricted by reality; a story in which events could not happen in real life, could take place in an imaginary world filled with magic

Tall tale: a story that uses exaggerations and humor to portray their characters; bigger than life because they perform superhuman feats;

an improbable, unusual, incredible or fanciful story

Mystery: a suspenseful story about a crime or some sort of puzzle to be solved presented as a novel play or movie

Drama: literary genre of works intended for the theater, intended for performance by actors on a stage, plays, musicals, etc.

Exercises:

A. Choose your favorite type of literature from the above list. Find a book at your library. Write a book report on this book for your teacher. Describe the setting; the characters; the time the story took place; the conflict within the story; the resolution of the conflict.

B. Choose a favorite character from this book and write a character study on this character: include why you like this character; a physical description of this character; what he did; what he said; how he felt; the effect he had on other characters.

7 Types of Poetry

Poetry is literature in metrical form. It is the creation and the expression of thoughts, ideas, and feelings in literature. It uses imagination to express the writer's personal feelings (through meaning, sound and rhythmic language choices) and brings to mind an emotional response from the reader. It often uses meter and rhyme but not necessarily. It is an authentic and individual mode of expression. In this chapter, the following types of poems will be covered: the **haiku**, the **limerick**, the **cinquain**, **biopoems**, **concrete poems**, and **free verse**.

Haiku is an ancient form of Japanese poetry that is usually made up of three lines. The first line has five syllables. The second line has seven syllables. And the third line has seven syllables. It contains a total of seventeen syllables. This brief poem is mainly about nature, feelings, and/or experiences. It has a 5-7-5 syllabic pattern.

Example: The sea hawk hunting

Sharp eyes and powerful claws

Designed for its prey

Example: A spark in the sun

Helps this tiny flower grow

Deep in the cool earth

Exercise: Now write two of your own haiku. Consider using topics from nature like: snowflakes, grasshoppers, love, frogs, family, etc. Brainstorm for ideas with your class.

_____

_____

_____

_____

_____

The **limerick** is often very funny verse. Originating in the Irish seaport of Limerick, Ireland, it is known to have been repeated by fishermen after a day's work, or by beggars and the working class. It has 5 lines in a rhyme scheme aabba; where the last word in lines 1, 2, and 5 rhyme and the final words in lines 3 and 4 rhyme.

Example: There was once a teacher, Mr. Kamara

Who married a thin, old witch named Sarah

They never knew if they were a pair

They never agreed on anything anywhere

Poor Mr. Kamara and the witch named Sarah

Example: There was once a fellow named Hall

He tripped, had a horrible fall

His wife was alarmed; he'd not come down

She hollered his name throughout the town

But he never heard the woman call.

Exercise: Now write two of your own limericks.

_____

_____

_____

_____

_____

_____

_____

_____

_____

_____

An American poet, Adelaide Crapsey was the creator of the first **Cinquain**. This form of poetry does not necessarily rhyme, as long it follows a specific pattern. It has five lines, and can be about any subject or topic.

line 1. -----one word---a noun which is the subject or title.

line 2. -----two words---adjectives describing the subject.

line 3. -----three words--verbs [action words] related to line one.

line 4. -----four words describing feelings about the subject.

line 5. -----one word [a synonym for the subject] as conclusion.

Example:

lions

powerful, furious

stalking, running, hunting

strong, impressive, trainable, territorial

carnivorous

Example:

diamonds

precious, valuable

grinding, cutting, crystalizing

sparkling, wedding, hard, gemstone

jewelry

Exercise: Now write your own cinquain.

_____

_____

_____

_____

_____

A **biopoem** is mainly about people. It is a biography in poem form. It has nine lines. It follows specific pattern as shown below:

Line 1. -----first name of person.

Line 2. -----four words that describe the person in line 1

Line 3. -----relative [e.g. sister, friend, teacher, mother, aunt]

Line 4. -----list three things he or she likes

Line 5. -----list three things about how he or she might feel.

Line 6. -----list three things he or she might be fearful about.

Line 7. -----list three things he or she might give away.

Line 8. -----name the place where he or she lives.

Line 9. -----last name or a statement about him or her

Example: Julliana

gorgeous, brilliant, outgoing, friendly

sister, Cathy

movies, pizza, cheerleading

jubilant, courageous, caring

rejection, snakes, lightning

candy, kisses, Christmas presents

Indianapolis

Morgan---my best friend in the family

Exercise: Now, write your own biopoem

Line 1. _____

Line 2. _____

Line 3. _____

Line 4. _____

Line 5. _____

Line 6. _____

Line 7. _____

Line 8. _____

Line 9. _____

Concrete poems take the shape of the object that is being described. First, you draw an outline of your object on a piece of paper. Next, make a list of words you intend to use to describe your subject. Finally, make sure that the words fit exactly along the line.

Pointing it guides us
Through forest & dell
We trust it. We must.
The arrow shows us
The route to take so
Lost we won't be when roaming about
Following its guidance
We do not
fail

Exercise: Now draw your subject/shape below on this page and write your concrete poem within it.

A **free verse** is a poem that has no specific restrictions or patterns. It is the expression of the feelings of the author. It can be about any subject or topic. It can rhyme or not. Lines can be short or long. It is a creative piece.

Examples: *(written by fourth graders at Southport Elementary School)*

GOALS

Goals are made for people to keep,
Not to throw out in a bulky heap,
Your goals can change, and that's alright,
But if they stay the same, that's a winning fight,
In the future you may receive,
Some goals you want to achieve,
Like being a record home-run hitter,
Or maybe a movie star,
No matter if your goals come true,
We will always have faith in you.

THE FUTURE

When it comes to what the future may bring,
We can only start imagining,
Whether we'll find a cure for all deadly diseases,
Or we'll find a permanent replacement for the human heart,
How will we travel to other planets? How will we play?

Just how will a person spend their day?
How will it change in the future that's near?
And is this change something to fear?
You'll never know.

There's always a change in technology and in race cars,

We'll probably make break-through in science and medicine,

Will population have more boys or girls?

Will the best music group be called the 'Pearls?'

What will happen, nobody knows,

I guess that's the way life always goes.

Exercise: Now, write your own free verse about any subject on this page.

_____

_____

_____

_____

_____

_____

_____

_____

_____

_____

_____

_____

_____

_____

8 Writing Strategies

There are various types of writing:

- **narrative:** writing about an event in a personal way, telling a story or part of a story

- **expository:** a type of writing where your purpose is to inform, explain, describe or define your subject to your reader. Your text will be meant to give information.

- **imaginative:** This type of writing is based on the writer's imagination. He may use hypothetical (imaginary) circumstances to solve a hypothetical problem. He is not limited by reality. This writing may include certain bits of fantasy.

- **descriptive:** uses concrete and specific details that appeal to one or more of the readers' five senses; these details about an object, place or person will be used to make the experience come alive for the reader.

Things to consider when writing:

1. Plan what you are going to write.

2. Stay on the topic or main idea.

3. Story should have a good beginning, a good middle, and a good ending.

4. Use strong verbs.

5. Use big words and vivid descriptions.

6. Use different and difficult sentence patterns.

7. Proofread for correct punctuation, capitalization, spelling, and grammar.

Exercise: These topics are suggestions for Parents, Teachers or Students to use for Creative Writing. Choose two or three of the following topics to write three or more paragraphs about each. Note that a paragraph is a group of sentences explaining a single idea. Usually, each paragraph is indented.

1. There was once a hermit in a house on a hill...

2. In a dusty crowded attic at old grandma's house I found...

3. The Runaway School Bus.

4. A Magic Race Car.

5. A Prehistoric Adventure.

6. When I was lying in bed last night, I heard footsteps in the attic...

7. My Favorite Relative.

8. If I had a million dollars...

9. Dreams.

10. Tell a story about someone you admire, and why.

11. What if animals could talk? With which animal would you talk, and about what would you talk?

12. Rewrite and use your own words for the song, "The Twelve Days of Christmas."

13. What if you woke up and discovered that you had been turned into a "THING" for one day. What "THING" would that be and what would you do for the day?

14. Finish the story "You would never believe what has just happened to me…"

15. Saturday, My Favorite Day of the Week.

16. The Boy Who Shrank.

17. The Horror at Camp Jellyjam.

18. A Foggy and Horrifying Night.

19. You just discovered an extinct animal in a cave. The animal has different body parts: head, tail, feet, torso, eyes, mouth and ears. Create its name by using the body parts names. Example: 'Hetafeebomar'! Draw your animal and describe a day with it.

20. I saw strange tracks in the snow leading towards my window…

21. Tell about the time when you were kind to someone.

22. Autumn is here and leaves are falling. Tell a story from the eyes of a leaf.

23. Describe an object without naming it.

24. Describe the happiest day of your life.

25. What if you could change places one day with your parents. What changes would you do at home?

26. Write a short story about a specific goal you would like to achieve in the year ahead.

27. You have the chance to make over a room in your house, what would you do?

28. If you could talk to Mother Nature about your wishes, what questions would you ask her?

29. Research about your favorite historical character, and write a summary about your findings.

30. The Windowless Red House on the Hilltop.

31. Write a play using characters in your classroom. Use the correct punctuation marks.

32. Write a tall tale about your best friend.

33. Create a recipe for a dish that's your family's favorite food.

34. You have just invented a time machine. Which time or era in the past or future would you visit first?

35. If you were the principal of your school for just one week, what would you do?

36. If you have lost someone special in your life and you had a chance to talk with them just one more time, what would you say?

37. Write an editorial about school life.

38. Write a fairy tale.

39. The most embarrassing thing that ever happened to me...

40. Write a fable.

41. If I had three wishes…

42. A gigantic creature came to my classroom today. He befriended me and we had a fun day. Tell about what you did together.

43. My Best Friend.

44. One foggy and an eerie Halloween night…

45. Lost in a Humongous Zoo.

46. Describe your vision of life 50 years from now.

47. I have a pet dinosaur…

48. Describe the most beautiful place you have ever seen.

49. If I could try three careers in the future, I would try…

50. What would happen if kids your age ruled the world?

51. The Story of My Life. Include all facts.

52. Is failure a better teacher than success? Why?

53. What three qualities do you look for in a friend? Describe them and tell why.

54. Give advice to a student who is coming up to your grade level next year.

55. Write a character sketch of your brother or sister or anyone you know very well.

56. If you were a turkey, what would you say to convince someone not to cook you for Thanksgiving dinner?

57. Write a story about what you did yesterday. But here is the twist: reverse the order of events beginning with the last event to the first.

58. Your best friend is moving to another city in different state. Write a farewell note for that friend.

59. Write a poem about your favorite family member using all the letters in their name. Example: Jen Just a girl Everyone loves Nothing special...

60. I'm afraid of _____ because _____

61. My friend and I were stranded on a dangerous remote island...

62. The Golden Snail.

63. Lost in Space.

64. I Encountered an Alien.

65. I visited an underwater school. You won't believe what I saw and experienced there!

66. Write a silly story in which every other word begins with a vowel.

67. You've invented a brand new product. Create an advertisement that will entice people to buy your product. What is the product? What does it do? How does it work? What is the cost? How do people get it? Where is it?

68. Be a television reporter who is reporting on the evening news about a fifth grade student who is so smart that he or she is now taking high school courses.

69. Express your opinion whether there is too much violence on television today.

70. I like all kinds of music except...

71. Describe snow to someone who has never seen snow before.

72. If I could solve any problem in the world today, I would…

73. If I could choose two famous people to spend the day with, they would be…

74. You are cleaning the basement of your house, and you found a very strange-looking bottle. You opened it. Describe what you found.

75. You have just been given $100,000 to spend. The only catch is that you cannot spend it on yourself. What would you do with the money?

76. Write a message for a time capsule. Tell about music, food, school, games and toys, and movies, etc. of your time period.

More Teacher Activities

Daily writing or Morning Work: Just for 10 minutes each day
Writing Activity with writing prompts to practice writing short paragraphs:

Exercise: Use the challenging synonyms listed for each small word in the title. On a separate piece of writing paper, compose a paragraph using different sentence patterns, vivid descriptions, strong verbs, and correct punctuations and spelling. Select a prompt of your choice.

A. **little**: tiny, microscopic, dwarf, pinch, petite, wee, miniature, diminutive.

Prompt: _____

Paragraph: Write a paragraph about your prompt using the synonyms above.

B. **beautiful**: glamorous, handsome, gorgeous, lovely, attractive, charming, elegant, fair, exquisite.

Prompt: _____

Paragraph: Write a paragraph about your prompt using the synonyms above.

C. **cloudy**: dark, dim, somber, overcast, murky, blurry, lightless, gloomy.

Prompt: _____

Paragraph: Write a paragraph about your prompt using the synonyms above.

D. **angry**: furious, annoyed, bitter, aggravated, vexed, infuriated, raged, provoked, irked, pestered

Prompt: _____

Paragraph: Write a paragraph about your prompt using the synonyms above.

E. **ask**: demand, question, request, inquire, implore, interrogate, query, beseech, petition

Prompt: _____

Paragraph: Write a paragraph about your prompt using the synonyms above.

F. **happy**: cheerful, upbeat, glad, lighthearted, joyful, merry, jubilant, gay.

Prompt: _____

Paragraph: Write a paragraph about your prompt using the synonyms above.

G. **rough**: bumpy, hard, tough, craggy, fuzzy, coarse, uneven, crude.

Prompt: _____

Paragraph: Write a paragraph about your prompt using the synonyms above.

H. **bother**: annoy, disturb, bore, hassle, harass, nag, upset.

Prompt: _____

Paragraph: Write a paragraph about your prompt using the synonyms above.

Reference Materials

Using **reference materials** will help you to research topics and find facts a lot easier. The following reference sources should give you direction as to where to look for information.

dictionary, encyclopedia, thesaurus, magazines, almanac, geographical dictionary, newspapers, atlas, biographical dictionary, Yellow Pages (phone book), White Pages (phone book), Guinness Book of Records, your search engine on your computer (Google, Yahoo Search, Dictionary.com, etc.)

Exercise: On the lines below, write the name of the reference materials you should use to find information about the following topics:

1. The address and phone number for McDonald's. _____

2. The pronunciation of a word. _____

3. The life cycle of a butterfly. _____

4. A garage sale where I can buy cheap things. _____

5. I need to know the longest river in the world. _____

6. To locate "Tibet" in East Asia. _____

7. First mountain climber to reach the peak of Mt. Everest. _____

8. I need to look for a job. _____

9. Research an Indian Tribe in South America. _____

10. Need quick facts about the Olympics in 2008. _____

11. Need to find words which mean the same as "huge. _____

12. Phone number and address of a friend. _____

13. I want to find out how to travel to Alaska. _____

14. I want to sell a house and I need to advertise it. _____

15. Need to find out who's the tallest person in the world. _____

16. I'm researching to compare the life of Abraham Lincoln to that of George Washington. _____

17. I want to check on the weather condition for today. _____

18. I want to read about the legendry "Babe Ruth" . _____

19. I need to locate a city in West Africa. _____

20. I'm doing a research work about rocks and minerals. _____

21. I want to research about the life history of Mother Theresa. _____

22. Which band is coming to town for a concert? _____

23. Want to know how many miles between Indianapolis and Washington, D. C. _____

24. Want to look up for the opposite word for "fantastic. _____

25. I want to find out how many entries are there for the meaning of the word 'spring'. _____

26. Need to find out about the causes, symptoms, and prevention of a specific disease. _____

27. I need to call for a tow truck to take my car to a mechanic. _____

28. I'm finding facts about the causes of volcanoes. _____

29. I suffer from asthma, and I want to know all about it. _____

30. What part of speech is the word: 'conservation'? _____

31. Want to study about the layers of the Earth. _____

Dictionary Skills

We use a **dictionary** for the following reasons:

A. Word definitions or meanings.

Example: the word 'change' may mean vary, transform, or alter.

B. Correct pronunciation of words.

The correct pronunciation of a word will usually just appear behind the entry word.

C. Correct spelling of a word.

The meaning is at the word's end.

D. The correct part of speech as used in a sentence.

A letter after a word indicates the part of speech to which the word belongs.

Example: the letter 'v' stands for a verb, 'n' stands for noun, 'adj' stands for adjective, 'adv' stands for an adverb, etc.

E. Sometimes the dictionary will give the synonyms and antonyms of words.

Example: far - distant, remote - near, close

F. The origin of word.

Some English words, that we use today, were borrowed from other languages from around the world. The letter 'F' after a word stands for French origin, the L stands for Latin origin, the OE stand for Old English, etc.

Example: 'cafeteria' has a French origin

'romance' has an Italian or Roman origin

Exercises:

A

Alphabetize the following common nouns by the first letter:

   birds, people, land, spacecraft, mountain, letter.

B

Alphabetize the following words by the second letters:

   good, game, grotesque, gifted, gum, gesture

C

Alphabetize the following words by the third letters:

   from, fruitful, frame, frigid, fret

D

Alphabetize the following words by the fourth letters

   fragile, frame, fracture, fraud, frail, fraternity

E

Alphabetize the following words by the fifth letter:

   stretch, stream, street, strewn, strep, strength

Exercise: To quickly locate a word in the dictionary, you use the first letter of the word. To show whether the word is at the beginning of the dictionary, between the letters 'A and H', put a '<u>B</u>' on the line. To show whether the word is in the middle of the dictionary, between the letters 'I and P', put an '<u>M</u>' on the line. To show whether the word is toward the end of the dictionary, between the 'Q and Z', put an '<u>E</u>' on the line.

1. ladder _____ 2. freedom _____ 3. zebra _____

4. tremendous _____ 5. brief _____ 6. tricycle _____

7. against _____ 8. demand _____ 9. wonder _____

10. cassava _____ 11. hilarious _____ 12. rest _____

13. effect _____ 14. solution _____ 15. baseball _____

16. tulip _____ 17. flower _____ 18. baggage _____

19. grapes _____ 20. jealous _____ 21. knife _____

22. introduce _____ 23 wrestle _____ 24. trumpet _____

Exercise: Using Guide Words

Guide words printed on the top of each page will help you to find the entry words you're looking for much quicker. The guide on the top left is the first word on the dictionary page, the guide word on the right is the last word on the dictionary page.

Below is a list of lettered words and some guide words. Write the pair of guide words that would appear on the line on the same page as the word.

Guide Words

grass - greatly	ripe - rock	green - grip
roll - rooster	gust - hair	rubber - rugged
dig - direction	runway - saddle	dirt - discover
butter - cactus	develop - dial	buoy - business
diary - difficult	cage - calm	camp - cap

1. dinosaur _____

2. roast _____

3. ruffle _____

4. cable _____

5. diagram _____

6. cake _____

7. grate _____

8. sack _____

9. grim _____

10. didn't _____

11. disappear _____

12. gorilla _____

13. burst _____

14. canned _____

15. irony _____

9 General Skills & Practice Test for Grammar

A.

Circle all the common nouns in each sentence.

Example: The mouse hid under the antique chair.
(because they name common objects)

1. The hyena laughed at the angry lion.

2. Few books were still standing on the shelf.

3. Twelve cookies were baking in the oven.

4. The sly fox told many stories to the other animals.

5. Many houses are destroyed during the high wind.

6. The pen and pencil on the table are missing.

7. I saw a grasshopper and an ant in the grass.

B.

Circle all the proper nouns in each sentence.

Example: (Jaclyn) prepared dinner for (Mary) and her friend (Frances).
(because they are names of people, and they are capitalized)

1. The Jones's left Indianapolis, Indiana for spring break in California.

2. Zachary predicted that Saturdays will come on certain days in June.

3. He rode a strong pony called "Kamara."

4. The fire show was planned for the "Fourth of July."

5. The Ohio River flows southwest of the Mississippi River.

6. Mt. Everest was first climbed by a British explorer.

7. Is Thanksgiving always in November?

8. The tourist group was made up of Americans, Germans, and Italians.

C.

Write the plural forms of each noun. Remember to review the rules for changing singular nouns to plural nouns.

1. band   _____   2. gas   _____

3. tomato   _____   4. bench   _____

5. ox   _____   6. wax   _____

7. buzz   _____   8. tax   _____

9. mouse _____ 10. captain _____

11. child _____ 12. deer _____

13. catch _____ 14. lunch _____

15. tooth _____ 16. dish _____

17. house _____ 18. sheep _____

19. key _____ 20. hero _____

21. woman _____ 22. calf _____

23. man _____ 24. country _____

25. stitch _____ 26. knife _____

27. truck _____ 28. igloo _____

29. month _____ 30. baby _____

D.
Write two words for each sentence, using the apostrophe, correctly showing ownership.

Example: The car is for John. <u>John's car</u>

1. The ball belongs to the boy. _____

2. The nose she bit belongs to Mrs. Creasy. _____

3. Those tiny legs are of Lindsey. _____

4. The purse was for Mrs. Jones. _____

5. The shoes in this store are for men. _____

6. Two fathers own the cars. _____

7. The home was built for girls. _____

8. That slick head belongs to Allen. _____

9. The fangs of a rattlesnake can inject enough poison to kill anyone.
_____

10. The wedding dresses belong to the ladies. _____

11. The bags belong to Georgina. _____

E.
Slash or put a line to separate the Subject and Predicate in each sentence.

Example: The teacher / is writing a book.

1. A football player scored a point.

2. My teacher dismissed the class.

3. Thomas Edison invented the electric bulb.

4. The fire truck skidded to a stop.

5. They chopped the trees around the house.

6. Cactus plants grow in deserts.

F.

Circle the (noun signal) or (noun determiner) in each sentence, and underline <u>the noun they signal</u>:

1. A rainbow is made up of seven colors.

2. Many people enjoy swimming.

3. The fierce fire burnt down several homes yesterday.

4. Only a few people saw the eclipse.

5. An eagle caught that rabbit.

6. Those horses were rounded up by some cowboys.

7. This street was paved by these workers.

G.

For the following adjectives list the word for the comparative and superlative form. Remember to review the rules and changes for this activity.

1. fancy   _____   _____

2. good   _____   _____

3. tall   _____   _____

4. handsome   _____   _____

5. nice   _____   _____

6. many   _____   _____

7. gorgeous _____ _____

8. fine _____ _____

9. bad _____ _____

10. breakable _____ _____

11. friendly _____ _____

12. big _____ _____

13. foolish _____ _____

14. hot _____ _____

15. angry _____ _____

16. beautiful _____ _____

17. heavy _____ _____

H.

Write: How? When? Where? on the line opposite each adverb to show which type.

1. slowly _____ 2. fast _____

3. downstairs _____ 4. out _____

5. then _____ 6. beneath _____

7. smartly _____ 8. frequently _____

9. soon _____   10. beyond _____

11. lazily _____   12. here _____

13. there _____   14. then _____

15. outside _____   16. in _____

17. now _____   18. tomorrow _____

I.

Underline the adjectives in each sentence:

1. Kelly is a more glamorous girl.

2. I'm very comfortable here.

3. The ugly alien that visited Earth has a shapeless head.

4. Tony is a careful chess player.

5. My friend is more talkative in class than I am.

6. She eats fine foods.

7. The speech was long and boring.

8. My sister is very active in drama.

J.

Underline the <u>diphthongs</u> that appear in some words in a sentence. Diphthongs are unique sounds that are made by the combination of mainly consonant letters with some vowels. These may include oi, oy, ow, ew, u.

1. Boiling water is not good for toys.

2. The couch was downtown in the city.

3. Few girls always participate in football games.

4. The big cow jumped over the cute girl.

K.

Circle the (diagraphs) that appear in certain words in a sentence. Diagraphs are unique sounds that are made by combining some consonant letters with vowels. These may include sh, ch, ph, th, gh.

1. The photographer took some shots of them together.

2. Allen's legs are chunkier than those of a chicken.

3. The whale was not too far from our boat nor the shore.

4. Ghosts are a traditional part of a Halloween celebration

5. His injured hands cannot catch the ball in the football game.

L.

Rewrite the correct form of the sentences below. They are wrong because they have double negatives:

1. I didn't know nothing about what happened on the playground.

_____

2. I'm not going nowhere with someone I barely know.

_____

3. I don't know nobody here.

_____

4. She doesn't have no money for shopping..

_____

5. None of the eggs won't hatch.

_____

M.

Put in the necessary punctuation marks in each sentence.

1. John said I am just tired and hungry

2. Dr. Jones looked at mary s teeth and said that they need cleaning

3. Well I stopped at the store and bought some eggs sugar milk and butter

4. Frances was born in Fort Wayne Indiana on November 11 1989

5. Who is your closest friend

6. Mom screamed put your toys away right now

7. Yes my dad works at burger king

N.

Write the abbreviations for the following words:

1. miss _____   2. captain _____

3. senior _____   4. street _____

5. January _____   6. governor _____

7. mister _____   8. general _____

9. missus _____   10. doctor _____

11.senior _____   12. president _____

13. road _____   14. February _____

15. Ohio _____   16. boulevard _____

17. lieutenant _____   18. Monday _____

19. superintendent _____   20. post office _____

21. avenue _____